WORD
BIBLICAL
THEMES

General Editor
David A. Hubbard

Old Testament Editor
John D. W. Watts

New Testament Editor
Ralph P. Martin

WORD
BIBLICAL
THEMES

1 and 2 Kings

T. R. HOBBS

ZONDERVAN
ACADEMIC

ZONDERVAN ACADEMIC

1 and 2 Kings
Copyright © 1989 by Word, Incorporated

Requests for information should be addressed to:
Zondervan, *3900 Sparks Dr. SE, Grand Rapids, Michigan 49546*

ISBN 978-0-310-11485-7 (softcover)

Library of Congress Cataloging-in-Publication Data

Hobbs, T. R. (T. Raymond)
    1 and 2 Kings: T. R. Hobbs.
      p. cm.
    Biography: p.
    Includes index.
    ISBN 978-0-849-90795-1
    1. Bible. O.T. Kings—Criticism, interpretations, etc. I. Title. II Title: First and
Second Kings. III. Series
    BS1335.2.H62 1989
    222'.506—dc20   89-16468

Unless otherwise noted, all Scriptures are from the Revised Standard version of the Bible. Copyright © 1952 [2nd edition 1971] by the Division of Christian Education of the National Council of the Churches of Christ in the United States of America. Used by permission. All rights reserved. Quotations indicated WBC are from the author's own translation in the Word Biblical Commentary, 2 Kings.

Printed in the United States of America

HB 08.14.2020

Dedicated to the Memory of
Michael Hobbs
(1939–1988)

CONTENTS

FOREWORD

Finding the great themes of the books of the Bible is essential to the study of God's Word, and to the preaching and teaching of its truths. But these themes or ideas are often like precious gems; they lie beneath the surface and can only be discovered with some difficulty. The large commentaries are most useful to this discovery process, but they are not usually designed to help the student trace the important subjects within a given book of Scripture.

The *Word Biblical Themes* meet this need by bringing together, within a few pages, all of what is contained in a biblical volume on the subjects that are thought to be most significant to that volume. A companion series to the *Word Biblical Commentary*, these books seek to distill the theological essence of the biblical books as interpreted in the more technical series and to serve it up in ways that will enrich the preaching, teaching, worship, and discipleship of God's people

The Books of Kings narrate that exciting and important period of Israel's history when kings and prophets walked the land. God was at work through them—sometimes, in spite of them. In this volume, Professor T. R. Hobbs has caught the heart of the writers' insights and allows us to share that vision and feel those convictions.

This volume is sent forth in the hope that it will contribute to the vitality of God's people, renewed by the Word and the Spirit and ever in need of renewal.

Southern Baptist Theological
Seminary
Louisville, Kentucky

John D. W. Watts
Old Testament Editor
Word Biblical Commentary

PREFACE

The books of 1 and 2 Kings comprise a masterful statement about the history of God with his people at a very important time in that history. From the end of the eleventh century B.C. to the early part of the sixth century B.C., Israel experimented with having a monarchy. These books cover a period slightly shorter than this.

Commentaries on the books of Kings (see, for example, WBC 12 and 13*) provide for a close and careful examination of the text, the language, the variant readings, the historical background, and the final construction of the narrative. That work is invaluable, and any serious student of this part of the Old Testament needs to wrestle with the same problems and issues with which the commentaries deal.

However, there is also great value in stepping back to examine the full canvas, and to sketch in broad strokes some of the major themes which emerge from a study of the books.

---

*Word Biblical Commentary, Volumes 12 and 13.

Not only is this of great value, but it is also a welcome task, and I am grateful to the Old Testament Editor of the *Word Biblical Commentary*, Dr. John D. W. Watts, for the invitation to tackle it.

In such a task one must always be wary of the danger of systematizing a work which was written in an ordered and disciplined, but unsystematic form. That is, the themes which I have chosen to expound in this volume are themes which I think are of value, and I think they are of value because they impress me as such when I read the text. Such a thematic approach is a perfectly sound method of biblical study—as long as one is aware of what one is doing. The danger is, of course, in supposing that such themes are all that can be said about the rich narrative of 1 and 2 Kings.

The narrative under discussion is a well-crafted one which rewards the readers each time they come to it seeking insight and understanding. It is a story of faithfulness and apostasy, of courage and cowardice, of remarkable wisdom and equally remarkable stupidity. Like all good stories it has its heroes and villains, but also like all good stories it often surprises the reader with the image reflected from its pages as if from a mirror. That is the genius of these books. That is also the way these books function as the Word of God. Like David listening to the story told by the outraged Nathan, we all too often fail to recognize our own reflection and we condemn too easily the faults and sins of others—faults and sins that we ourselves could rightly own. It is my hope that the readers of this small volume will be encouraged by its pages to read again the books it seeks to expound.

No writer on the books of Kings can be unaware of the contribution made to his or her understanding of the short, but effective, work of Jacques Ellul, *The Politics of God and the Politics of Man*.[1] Ellul concentrated on 2 Kings, and brought to bear on the book his understanding of politics and theology. He developed an approach quite different from the one we will take. Ellul chose to concentrate on various characters and has provided a very valuable and stimulating study which is to be recommended.

A number of people have encouraged and assisted me in the writing of this study, and deserve my thanks. This book was completed during the first part of a sabbatical leave, and I would like to thank the principal of McMaster Divinity College, Dr. Melvyn Hillmer, as well as the senate and board of trustees for providing the opportunity to concentrate on writing for an extended period of time. My colleague, Dr. Stuart Frayne, Hurlburt Professor of Preaching at Mc-Master Divinity College, read the completed manuscript and from his wisdom, experience, and common sense made numerous suggestions for improvement. For this act of kindness I am very grateful. Any errors and clumsiness of style that remain are entirely my responsibility.

Two items of information are in order concerning certain abbreviations used in this volume: (1) References in the text which refer to the companion volumes in the *Word Biblical Commentary* are abbreviated, e.g., WBC 12:322, indicating a reference to Volume 12, p. 322. Volume 12 is 1 Kings in the *Word Biblical Commentary*, and Volume 13 is 2 Kings. (2) In some instances, verse numbers in the Hebrew Bible differ from those in English versions. When such a reference is cited, the Hebrew enumeration will be given first, followed by the English verse number(s) in brackets.

In the early stages of the writing of this book my brother, Michael Hobbs, died of cancer. I loved him and will miss him, and to his fond memory this book is dedicated.

T. R. Hobbs
McMaster University

1 INTRODUCTION

The perspective of 1 and 2 Kings

The division between 1 and 2 Kings is quite artificial and occurred relatively late in the books' history. The material from the first chapter of 1 Kings to the last of 2 Kings should be treated as one literary unit. As we shall see, it is a composition using information from many sources, but in its final form it is a unity. In Jewish tradition, this part of what Christians know as the Old Testament has been designated part of the "Former Prophets," and modern critical scholarship has seen Kings as part of the "deuteronomistic history." What do these terms mean? What relationship do these books, which are usually seen as "history," have to the prophets? Further, what do 1 and 2 Kings have to do with the book of Deuteronomy?

First, it will be helpful to note the differences between 1 and 2 Kings, and those parts of the books of Chronicles which cover the same period of Israelite and Judaic history. The books of Chronicles are concerned with different

1

aspects of the same history—the origin and development of religious ritual and religious personnel in that history. For example, a comparison of the two accounts of the reform of Josiah (2 Kgs 22, 23; 2 Chr 34, 35) shows that the Chronicles account pays far more attention to the role of the priests in the reform, and the practice of the Passover, which Josiah reinstated in Jerusalem. Further, the reign and reform of Hezekiah (2 Kgs 18-20; 2 Chr 29-32) is treated in a similar fashion by the chronicler. Such comparisons clearly show the emphasis of the chronicler, but what of the writer of 1 and 2 Kings?

It is important to note what the chronicler omits in his retelling of the accounts of 1 and 2 Kings, which he probably had before him when he wrote. Nothing is found in Chronicles of the activities of the great prophets of Israel. No mention is made of the role of Isaiah in the reign of Hezekiah. And, most important of all, nothing of the activities of the great prophets Elijah and Elisha is found in Chronicles. This omission throws into sharp focus their presence in such a large part of 1 and 2 Kings. So, a major difference between the two accounts is that the writer of 1 and 2 Kings includes much more material about the prophets in his history.

But we can say more. Beyond the stories *about* prophets, the writer of 1 and 2 Kings tends to look at the history he is writing from the prophetic point of view. Prominent in his scheme of things is the Word of God, uttered by the prophet. It often determines the history that follows. The same concern for correct worship of God, for proper treatment of society's marginalized persons, that is found in the poetry of the prophets is also found in 1 and 2 Kings. This double emphasis—on the stories about prophets on the one hand, and the historic role of the prophets on the other—provides 1 and 2 Kings with a distinct prophetic flavor.

But what does Kings have to do with Deuteronomy? After all, that is surely the source of the term *deuteronomistic*. The same material designated "Former Prophets" (Joshua through 2 Kings) in Jewish tradition is called deuteronomistic history (often Dtr for short) for reasons of literary style and presentation. Literary style is, of course, often a difficult thing to detect, but it is not impossible. The book of Deuteronomy, for example, has long been regarded as distinct from the rest of the Pentateuch because of its marked style. It tends to be pedantic and to have a Hebrew dialect which can be called crude. Its sentences are relatively short and there is a tendency to use the same words, or clusters of words, over and over again. (The reader is referred to the works of Driver and Weinfeld for several examples of the style.)[1]

In addition to this, the book of Deuteronomy is presented as one long speech of Moses. Unlike the other books of the Pentateuch, action is kept to a minimum. Instead, ideas are presented, usually in a homiletic or didactic manner. In Deuteronomy, Moses persuades, cajoles, threatens, and encourages with the spoken word. In the deuteronomistic history as a whole, and in 1 and 2 Kings in particular, speeches, spoken prayers, or editorial comments accomplish the same purpose. Further, it is in these speeches—e.g., Joshua's at Shechem (Josh 23, 24) or Samuel's at Mizpah (1 Sam 8), or prayers (e.g., Solomon's at the dedication of the temple, 1 Kgs 8), or prophetic comments (2 Sam 7; 1 Kgs 18), or other important comments (1 Kgs 4; 9)—that the deuteronomistic tendencies of the history become clear.

But beyond this, when Israel and Judah are seen going into exile, the evaluation of the history at that point bears remarkable similarity to the judgments found in the book of Deuteronomy. Deuteronomy 4 and 28 anticipate the apostasy, judgment, and exile of the people. And the reforms carried out by Josiah (2 Kgs 22, 23) have long been recognized as dependent upon the standards set down in Deuteronomy.

What does this tell us about the author of 1 and 2 Kings (and indeed of the whole deuteronomistic history)? He is a

3

"deuteronomist" insofar as he sees in the book of Deuteronomy the standards which the people of Israel and Judah must maintain in their public and religious lives in order to be called the people of God, and to remain bound to him in covenant. This does not mean, of course, that the other books of the Pentateuch are unimportant, any more than the choice of one particular Christian theologian over another as one's favorite, means that the others are of no value. It was simply the author's decision that the message of Deuteronomy, exemplified in the history of the people, needed to be heard again.

Sources

The writer did not just sit down and write a story. He chose instead to compile a cohesive narrative of the history of his people, which would demonstrate the validity of the principles set out in the book of Deuteronomy. To be true to the past he needed to rely on known contemporary understandings of the past, and to be true to his overall task he needed to offer his readers a narrative worth reading. To accomplish the first part of this task he used many extant literary sources—like any good historian—and also traditions about the past. It will be helpful for an understanding of the work to mention some of these sources.

Undoubtedly our writer was dependent upon written records from archival sources. He was writing during the Exile (ca. 500 B.C.). To give some perspective to the material he is dealing with, he was removed one hundred years from Josiah, two hundred years from Hezekiah, three hundred years from Elijah and Elisha, and four hundred from the reign of Solomon. As in most ancient Near Eastern centralized bureaucratic administrations, records were kept in Israel and Judah, and must have been used for the kind of historical narrative we find in 1 and 2 Kings. These records would include incidents from the reigns of former kings, matters of foreign policy, records from the original building and subsequent repairs of the temple. The beginning of 1 Kings (chs 1, 2) is seen by many scholars as the conclusion to the "Throne Succession Story" of King David's reign. It has also been argued that at times the writer lapses into a detectable archival style, thus betraying the source of his information. Be that as it may, the narrative of 1 and 2 Kings is no haphazard or fanciful creation, but is in part a careful compilation from a variety of official sources.

The writer's familiarity with the prophetic tradition shows he also had access to the stories about the prophets. The precise relationship between the account of Hezekiah's reign in 2 Kings 18–20 and the account of the same events in Isaiah 36–38 is difficult to determine, but our writer was fully aware of the role of this major prophet in these critical events in Judah's history.

He was familiar enough, too, with those prophetic circles that had preserved the stories of the deeds of the two great prophets Elijah and Elisha. These stories had been preserved and were undoubtedly retold as inspiration to others who followed in their steps, so that by the time of the prophet Amos (ca. 750 B.C.) there was already a consciousness of standing in the tradition of "[Yahweh's] servants the prophets" (Amos 3:7).

Alongside the stories of these major figures are brief anecdotes of the activities of other prophets—Ahijah of Shiloh (1 Kgs 11:29–39), the anonymous prophet from Judah (1 Kgs 13), Jonah ben Amittai (2 Kgs 14:25)—and the overall impression is of a story unfolding according to the Word of God through the prophets. Other material of a nonarchival nature, such as the tradition of Solomon's gift of wisdom (1 Kgs 3) and the visit of the Queen of Sheba (1 Kgs 10), was also used.

The matter of the unity of the books of 1 and 2 Kings is vigorously debated among scholars, and centers around the

5

so-called double redaction of the deuteronomistic history. This is the theory that there was an original deuteronomistic history written during the reign of Josiah, and that this version was edited and expanded during the period of the Exile. The purpose of the new edition was to take account of the events that followed the death of Josiah. Readers of DeVries's commentary on 1 Kings (WBC 12:lii) will note that he allows for a considerable number of "postdeuteronomistic additions" to the text of 1 Kings, which included "instructional" and "ideological" material. In my work on 2 Kings (WBC 13:xxii–xxv), I found that the number of such additions was minimal and unimportant. My position then, as now, is that the arguments for an earlier edition of the history written during the reign of Josiah, have not been persuasive.

Such differences in matters of scholarly opinion will persist. Ancient books were not protected by copyright or anything like it, and in some cases there is strong evidence for additions being made to a biblical book. An example of this is Jeremiah 52, which is almost an exact copy of 2 Kings 24:18–25:30, and which comes after the statement "Thus far are the words of Jeremiah" (Jer 51:64). This should not be interpreted in a negative way. The fact that a document is reinterpreted by later generations of readers testifies to the power of the work and of its message.

Structure

Like style, structure is sometimes a subjective matter, and what one interpreter sees as structure, another will not. Structure is often something which we impose on a text to help us in our reading of it. Ancient literature is not always easy to read. Its literary conventions are not those with which the twentieth-century reader is familiar. The tendencies in Hebrew narrative to switch subjects arbitrarily, to avoid descriptive passages, and to use repetition can be confusing, so it is helpful if the reader can put the narrative into some kind of recognizable framework. However, in such an exercise, we must always bear in mind that this framework is what the reader sees, not necessarily what the writer consciously intended.

The opening chapters of 2 Kings continue the story of the prophetic presence in Israel with the depiction of Elijah's departure and the succession of Elisha. The chapters are in the form of what some interpreters call an "inversion," or, to use the more technical phrase, an extended chiasmus. This is a device in which ideas, words, and themes are repeated in reverse order and in a different setting. It is the opinion of some that the whole of 1 and 2 Kings is constructed in this way; that there is a progression from Solomon, through the division of the kingdom and the local wars, through the reigns of Omri and Ahab, and into the activities of the great prophets Elijah and Elisha. Here a turning point comes in the narrative and previous events are now mirrored, as the fortunes of Israel and Judah are reversed and the steps are retraced though the reigns of Hezekiah and Josiah until the land is lost and the grandeur of Solomon's reign and the size of his territory are nothing but a memory. There is value in this hypothesis, and since we are attempting to sketch the large picture rather than the small details, it might be helpful for the reader to bear this pattern in mind

Historical background

The historical background of a book such as 1 or 2 Kings is important as an aid to understanding. It does not tell us everything we need to know about an author, but it does help fill in some of the necessary detail. Here we make a distinction between the writer's own historical background

The Monarchy in Israel/Judah

B.C.	EGYPT	JUDAH	ISRAEL	ARAM	MESOPOTAMIA
	XXII Dyn	Solomon (960–927)			
930					
	Shishak (925)	Rehoboam (926–910)	Jeroboam (927–906)		
920 910		Abijah (909–907) Asa (906–878)	Nadab (905–904) Baasha (903–882)		
900 890				← Ben Hadad I	
880		Jehoshaphat (877–853)	Elah (881–880) Zimri Omri (879–869)		
870			Ahab (868–854)	← Ben Hadad II	
860				Qarqar (853)	← Shalmaneser III
850 840		Jehoram (852–841) Ahaziah (840) Athaliah (839–833)	Ahaziah (853–852) Jehoram (851–840) Jehu (839–822)	← Hazael	
830		Joash (832–803)			
820			Jehoahaz (821–805)		← Adad Nirari III
810		Amaziah (802–786)	Jehoash (804–789)		
800 790			Jeroboam (788–748)		
		Uzziah (785–760)			
780 770 760		Jotham (759–744)			

B.C.	EGYPT	JUDAH	ISRAEL	ARAM	MESOPOTAMIA
750	XXIII Dyn				
			Zechariah (747) Shallum (747)		Tiglath-pileser
740		Ahaz (743–728)	Menahem (746–735)	Rezin	
			Pekahiah (735–734) Pekah (734–731)		
730			Hoshea (730–722)		
		Hezekiah (727–699)			Shalmaneser V
					←— Sargon II
			Fall of Samaria (722)		
720 710					
700	Tirhakah (?)	←——————————————————			—Sennacherib
		Manasseh (698–644)			
690 680 670					Esarhaddon
660 650	←—————————————————————————————————				Asshurbanipal
		Amon (643–642) Josiah (641–610)			
640 630 620					
610	Necho—————→	Jehoahaz (609) Jehoiakim (608–598)			
600		Jehoiachin ← (598) Zedekiah (598–586)			
590					——Nebuchadrezzar
		Fall of Jerusalem←			
580 570					

these dates are approximate and based on the newly developed chronological scheme of J. H. Hayes and P. K. Hooker in *A New Chronology for the Kings of Israel and Judah*.[2] In the above chart, only those foreign rulers who threatened Israel and Judah with invasion are listed. The arrows show the origins and approximate times of invasions of, or attacks upon, Judah and Israel during the time of the monarchy.

and the background of the events he describes. In the first case, it is clear that the books were completed during the Exile of Judah in Babylon. The last events described in Kings provide us with the necessary clue for this. Jerusalem had been sacked twice in just over a decade, during the reign of Jehoiakim (597 B.C.) and again during the reign of his successor, Zedekiah (586 B.C.). The royal family had been taken into exile with the leading citizens of the land; and all that was important to Judah—temple, king, land—had been lost. The writer, who must have experienced these last events, tries to make sense of this tragedy in terms of the religious traditions of his people, which included the Exodus, the Law-giving at Sinai, and the covenant. As Robert Polzin has expressed it:

> It is as though the Deuteronomist is telling us in Deuteronomy, "Here is what God has prophesied concerning Israel," but in Joshua-2 Kings, "This is how God's word has been exactly fulfilled in Israel's history from the settlement to the destruction of Jerusalem and the Exile."[3]

This story begins with the close of the reign of David (1 Kgs 1, 2). What follows is a history of the monarchy in Israel and Judah. It is a history of great promise under Solomon, the wise temple-builder and architect of a powerful administrative empire. But it is also a story of a promise squandered, as ideals are lost. Both commentaries provide detailed analyses of questions of history as well as a chronology of the period from Solomon (ca. 960 B.C.) to the close of the monarchy (586 B.C.), so there is no need to repeat the details here. Instead, the chart on pages 8-9 provides a general guide to the fortunes of Israel and Judah during this period. The arrows indicate periods and direction of political and military pressure

The books of 1 and 2 Kings stand in their own right as a major part of the deuteronomistic history. In fact, they form the climactic ending to the whole story of God's history with his people up to the time of writing. Beyond this, the books also form a source of information for the later work of the writer of 1 and 2 Chronicles.

Undoubtedly, the tradition of Solomon's wisdom and the achievements of the courtiers of Hezekiah have influenced the formation of the book of Proverbs (Prov 25:1), as well as other parts of the Wisdom Tradition. Within the context of the prophetic tradition and the literature which emerged from it, found now in what is known as the "Latter Prophets" (Isaiah through Malachi), these books provide a series of historical examples of the force of the prophetic word. One can imagine as one listens to the preaching of Amos or Hosea, Jeremiah or Isaiah, that standing in the shadows nodding approval are the ghosts of Elijah and Elisha. The same concerns for the less fortunate, for moral responsibility of leaders, and for the proper understanding of history as God's history, are present throughout the prophetic tradition. Indeed, the figure of Elijah, like that of Moses, enters into the hopes of that tradition as the coming kingdom of God is anticipated (Mal 3:24 [4:5]).

In the eschatological hopes of sections of Judaism in the period we know as the "intertestamental period," both Elijah and Moses continue their roles as harbingers of the coming kingdom. But for us it is the influence of 1 and 2 Kings on the New Testament that is most important. In the New Testament, some of the same interests we find in the Old Testament are present, while others have undergone some transformation. One might expect Jesus, who was raised as a first-century Jew, to use in his teachings illustrations from the Hebrew Scriptures, and he does—

but from a different perspective. For example, Solomon, rather than being seen as an example of wisdom, is used by Jesus as an example of ostentation (Matt 6:29).

In the Gospels, Jesus is portrayed as patterning much of his ministry on that of the prophets, particularly the work of Elijah and Elisha. In the transfiguration of Jesus, as recorded in the opening verses of Mark 9, Jesus is accompanied by two prophetic giants, Moses and Elijah. He acknowledges openly the role of Elijah played by John the Baptist (Matt 11:13; Mark 9:11-13). His concern for widows (Luke 7:11-17), for Gentiles (Mark 7:24-30), and for the hungry (Mark 6:30-44) reflects the concerns of both Elijah and Elisha. That these two prophets influenced his understanding of his ministry is seen most clearly in Luke 4:24-27, in which he holds them up as models of concern. The Letter to the Hebrews sums up the impact of the narratives of Elijah and Elisha, among others, when it lists those past heroes of the faith who

. . . through faith conquered kingdoms, enforced justice, received promises, . . . escaped the edge of the sword, won strength out of weakness, became mighty in war, put foreign armies to flight. Women received their dead by resurrection. (Heb 11:33-34)

2　KINGS

The role of kings in Israel

Much of the narrative of Kings is taken up with stories of varying lengths about the kings of the united Israel and the kings of the separate nations of Israel and Judah. But to understand the richness of this narrative we need to step back a little into the early history of the monarchy.

The historical beginnings of kingship in Israel are given to us earlier in the deuteronomistic history, in 1 Samuel 1–12, with its story of the transition and transformation of Israel from a tribal society to a monarchy. This transition was a diffi- cult one because it meant some major changes for Israel in her political and social structures and in her understanding of her relationship with God. The difficulties, both anticipated and experienced, are found mirrored in Samuel's reaction to the original request by the elders for a king. The reaction is at first negative and kingship is judged as a rejection of God's king- ship (1 Sam 8:6–9). But eventually Samuel acquiesces to the move and at the command of God grants the elders' request.

The story of the request for a king, especially in 1 Samuel 8–12, has been the subject of much scholarly debate, and most of the debate has centered around the question of a double view of kingship in these chapters. Many believe that this double view, with a positive and negative element, reflects the original literary sources used by the deuteronomist, one with a positive outlook on monarchy, and one with a negative one. This is entirely possible. The subsequent history of the monarchy shows that both attitudes were present throughout. Some prophets, for example Isaiah, accepted the institution of kingship and worked within its framework (Isa 7:1–17; 11:1–16), whereas others, such as Hosea, found the institution a hindrance to the people's understanding of God (Hos 5:1; 7:7; 8:4).

It is also important, however, to see what the final effect of this narrative is. It is not a clumsy collection of sources with conflicting viewpoints, but a clever portrayal of the opposing reactions to kingship which would have evolved at the time. Such a move would not necessarily have met with universal approval since so many had so much to lose as well as gain. The narrative of the monarchy's founding reflects the ambivalence which greeted it.

Forms and models for kingship were available throughout the ancient Near East at this time, and the elders certainly wished to take advantage of what those forms had to offer by way of a style of ruling. After all, they wanted a king "like all the nations" (1 Sam 8:5). At the same time, each nation's version of kingship was unique to that nation. And while comparisons are helpful, to complete the picture we also need to look at the distinctive features of Israelite kingship.

What kingship offered Israel was on the one hand "more taxes, military conscription, arbitrary police, the impossibility of limiting power,"[1] and even the danger of the "repaganization of Israel."[2] And it is clear that there are dangers in the move, as Samuel so clearly points out (1 Sam 8:10-14). But, on the other hand, the introduction of kingship also offered new opportunities for worship and understanding. Monarchy was rationalized for two very good reasons. First, there was a serious military threat (the Philistines) to the very life of Israel. Second, the old regime represented by Samuel's sons was corrupt and not up to dealing with the new challenge.

In practical terms, monarchy meant a centralization of power in one person and his administration. This, it seems, was the price which the elders were willing to pay for security and safety (1 Sam 8:19-22). Connected to this centralization of power was the development of a symbolic center, Jerusalem, in which a new theology was born. The symbols included the temple, the palace, and the trappings of monarchy, together with the ideological support known as the "David-Zion traditions."

These are the religious ideas which became associated with the new institution. They provide a new focus for the notions of God's faithfulness, election of Israel, and protection of his people (e.g., Ps 2). They also offer support for the new institution and give it validity. These traditions find their clearest form in the covenant with David, which has its first exposition in 2 Samuel 7, but is expanded and restated in Psalms 89, 110, and 132, among others. The covenant captures the essence of the importance of the new institution. David (and his successors) are chosen by God as a symbol of his faithfulness. David is promised (not unconditionally) a continuing dynasty in Jerusalem.

But this new opportunity also presents a new challenge. The deuteronomist's history of the period of the judges is hardly a flattering one, and already an early experiment with kingship had failed (Judg 8:22-9:57). Stability had come with Samuel, but cannot continue. The unspoken question is, can the new institution of monarchy preserve and perpetuate the

15

old covenant values? Will the difference between authority and despotism be maintained? Will kingship succeed?

Kings and Torah

One of the distinguishing features of Israelite kingship is its relationship to the *Torah* (lit: "instruction." This term captures the broader concept much better than the more common translation, "Law.") Ancient Near Eastern nations such as the Hittites, the peoples of Mesopotamia, all had "law-codes" dealing with the daily life of their citizens—regulating matters of property, relationships, management of resources, and sexual access. But whereas these other law-codes have come down to us with the names of kings attached—the Lipit-Ishtar Code, the Hammurabi Code, the Laws of Eshnunna—the Torah of Israel is always "the Torah of Moses." Its originator was not a king, but one who spoke with God face to face, and who is remembered not as a ruler, but rather as a prophet (Deut 18:18). This places the Israelite king's relationship to the Torah and to God on an entirely different footing than that of the kings of neighboring nations. He is not the proclaimer of the Torah, but is himself under its rule. As one scholar has put it, "the king's power was not unrestrained and was repeatedly checked by the terms of God's covenant with his people."[3]

Deuteronomy, which acts as a prologue to the deuteronomistic history, anticipates this in chapters 16–18, particularly in Deuteronomy 17:14–20 with the so-called Torah of the king. But again, this is not a torah *from* the king, but a torah which regulates the behavior of the king. It is interesting to note in 1 Samuel 8:11 that Samuel describes the possible behavior of a despotic king as "the *mishpat* of the king." This is the word which elsewhere in the Old Testament is often translated "judgment." There might be a touch of irony here, almost as if Samuel is saying, "This is how a king will be judged."

With this in mind, it seems plausible that the "rights and duties of the kingship" (1 Sam 10:25) which Samuel gave to the people have something to do with this "royal torah." In 2 Kings 11:12, when the Davidic monarchy was restored after a brief interval, Jehoash is given "testimonies" at his coronation. This is a legal term, and possibly refers to the same thing.

Another aspect of the monarchy in Israel, at least in the case of David (2 Sam 5:1-5), Rehoboam (1 Kgs 12:1-20), and the restored Jehoash (2 Kgs 11:4), is that the reign of a king is negotiated with the elders and representatives of the people. In 2 Kings 11:14, these negotiations are called a "covenant," and covenants have stipulations or regulations governing them. It is clear that there are some limits on the monarchy in Israel, and recently some scholars have argued that Deuteronomy 16–18 forms a kind of constitution of the monarchy, that is, the conditions under which a king would be allowed. To be noted is that his power is not absolute. It is to be shared by judges, priests, and prophets.

The royal Torah in Deuteronomy 17:14-20 and Samuel's exposition of it in 1 Samuel 8:10-18 have reminded many interpreters of Solomon, but the image here is of any king in Israel, or in the ancient Near East in general. Here is described the potential for abuse and the costs of the new system. Deuteronomy 17:14-20 expressly prohibits abuse in terms of self-aggrandizement and too many marriage alliances with foreign nations. The counter to abuse is the copy of "this torah" which he is to keep before him.

In 2 Samuel 7, we find the covenant with David and his successors. The Lord will provide David with a "house" (i.e., dynasty; note the play on words). David and his successors will be corrected and punished if they sin (v 14), yet God's faithfulness will remain. More than once in the ongoing history of the monarchy these sentiments are repeated in thoroughly deuteronomistic language. In 1 Kings 2:1-4 David's last words to Solomon include the admonition to obey the Torah of Moses, that the promise of God might be fulfilled. In 1 Kings 9:1-9, further exposition is found in God's response to Solomon. Here, not only is the fate of the monarchy in the balance (vv 4, 5), but also the possibility of exile of the entire people is raised (vv 6-9).

To summarize, the limitations of kingship in Israel entail the king's submission to the Torah, exclusive worship of God, and proper treatment of the people.

Royal examples

If Polzin's characterization of the relationship of Deuteronomy to the deuteronomistic history is correct (see Introduction), then the narrative of 1 and 2 Kings will provide many illustrations of how this is worked out in the history of Israel and Judah. However, we should be aware that although Polzin is correct when the entire history is viewed from beginning to end, when the reader begins at 1 Kings 1 there is a slightly different perspective. Given what we know of the beginnings of kingship in Israel, when we begin to read the opening sentences of 1 Kings we cannot claim the omniscience of the author, but we are faced instead with the question of how the ensuing history will expound the principles of Deuteronomy.

The simplest answer is, of course, by telling a story. But this is a story with its own literary conventions, which are not immediately recognizable to the modern reader. To our eyes the treatment of the material appears uneven, repetitive, and arbitrary. But, if we take it on its own terms we find it to be a richly textured story, with no small measure of irony. We also find that on occasion the writer invites us to pause with him and examine the characters of the kings in more detail. This practice of slowing down the pace of a narrative, so that a relatively short incident is given long coverage, is a literary device which some have called "retardation." It is obvious that the writer devotes a lot of space to some kings and little to others. This does not mean that those given small coverage are any less important, but rather that those on whom he dwells are particularly appropriate for illustrating his main themes. The space devoted to them gives him opportunity to develop their characters by describing the actions they perform. Let us look at a selection of the kings he treats.

1 and 2 Kings begins with the close of the reign of *David* (1 Kgs 1, 2). This section is regarded by many as a "succession narrative," an account of the reasons why Solomon became king after David—after all, he was not the oldest of David's sons. The David we encounter here is not the David of the early days. Instead he is an old and weak man (1 Kgs 1:1). He is ignorant of the affairs of his court (1 Kgs 1:11), and he is manipulated by both Nathan and Bathsheba (1 Kgs 1:12-27). Finally he takes some measure of control (1 Kgs 1:28-37), and offers his charge to Solomon (1 Kgs 2:1-9) before he dies. But the main actors in these opening chapters are Nathan, Bathsheba, and Solomon. In fact, it is to the success of Solomon that these chapters direct us.

Solomon has more space devoted to him in 1 and 2 Kings than any other king except David, and the reasons for this are several. First, because of all he accomplished it is likely that there were more records from the reign of Solomon than any subsequent king. Second, in the writer's scheme of things the succession of Solomon was very important for showing in no uncertain terms the fulfillment of the promise of 2 Samuel 7. Third, the ultimate story of Solomon provided a perfect illustration of the writer's theological viewpoint.

The lesson of Solomon is one which was emphasized very early in the negotiations for monarchy. Solomon did indeed accomplish a great deal. He won a civil war and overcame a challenge to his succession (1 Kgs 1, 2). As king, he set out to build the temple in Jerusalem (1 Kgs 6) and when that was completed he then built a large palace complex for his court (1 Kgs 7). He gained wisdom (1 Kgs 3), developed trade throughout his empire, and became known throughout the world for his wealth and wisdom (1 Kgs 4, 10). But this narrative from 1 Kings 1-10 is almost a setup for the fall which followed. A simple but vital principle was given early in the history of kingship, when Samuel was tempted to anoint the most physically impressive of Jesse's sons. God said,

"Do not look on his appearance or on the height of his stature, because I have rejected him; for the Lord sees not as man sees; man looks on the outward appearance, but the Lord looks on the heart." (1 Sam 16:7)

It is the heart, the will of Solomon which is turned away to other gods by the wives he married for political reasons (1 Kgs 11:4). He died, not famous, or universally known, but as an apostate. His kingdom is threatened, and the dark side of the covenant promise, the side of judgment, now reveals itself.

In the stories of *Rehoboam* and *Jeroboam*, Solomon's successors, it is this theme which is illustrated. Rehoboam wrecked the negotiations for the royal covenant with Israel by listening to the "young men" who spurned the advice of the elders of Israel and led the king to abuse his people with harsh slave labor (1 Kgs 12). Jeroboam, like all headstrong revolutionaries, was motivated initially by the welfare of his people, but eventually led them into deeper and deeper apostasy (1 Kgs 12, 13).

By the time of *Omri* and *Ahab*, the rift between the representatives of God and the will of the king had become deep. In all the confrontations between the house of Omri and the prophet of the Lord, the king broke the covenant law (1 Kgs

21:1-15) and despised the word of God given by the prophet (1 Kgs 22:5-28), only to finally fall victim to judgment (1 Kgs 22:29-36). The same pattern is echoed later by the Judean Jehoiakim in his confrontations with the prophet Jeremiah (Jer 36).

Hezekiah (2 Kgs 18-20), like Solomon, began well. He introduced worship reforms in Jerusalem, and rid the city of many practices of Canaanite worship. But he faltered when Sennacherib invaded (2 Kgs 19:1-7), and consequently became sick with a symbolic skin disease (2 Kgs 20:1-11). He also allowed a potential enemy a foretaste of the temple and palace treasures when he showed them off to Babylonian visitors (2 Kgs 20:12-19).

Finally, there is Josiah (2 Kgs 22:1-23:30) who, like Hezekiah, did so well with his reforms, and his rebellion against Assyria. Of Josiah it is said that he was unequaled in virtue—yet he died a tragic and untimely death at Megiddo (2 Kgs 23:28-30).

Each of these portraits is done with skill and subtlety, and each serves as an illustration of the growing apostasy of the people of Israel and Judah, led by their kings. Ellul is correct in stating that such presentations are not for imitation. But neither are they simply for reading. They are, rather, for meditation because in each of these kings is found an attitude of the human heart.

In the final analysis

Throughout Kings the writer repeats a formula of evaluation, either "he did evil in the eyes of the Lord" or "he did what was right in the eyes of the Lord." This formula recalls the standards by which these kings were to be evaluated, not human standards but divine ones. It also, incidentally, sets the limits to what we can know of these kings, because the writer uses only that which illustrates this perspective.

Although the formula is used of almost every king and sounds almost mechanical, it is, in fact, used in a subtle way which has important consequences for our theological understanding of 1 and 2 Kings. In the first place, all the kings of the northern nation of Israel who are evaluated are judged to be apostates. There is one king, Hoshea, who is damned with the faint praise that he is not as bad as his predecessors (2 Kgs 17:2). And there are two, Zimri and Shallum, who are not judged at all (1 Kgs 16:1-13; 2 Kgs 15:13-15), no doubt due to their remarkably short reigns. But the rest are damned. And for each, the fault is that of following in the sins of Jeroboam ben Nebat, who at the beginning of the separate history of Israel deliberately set her on a course of apostasy. For Jeroboam, rejection of the house of David (1 Kgs 12:16) meant rejection of David's God as well.

There is a biblical principle, expounded by the writer of 1 and 2 Kings, that the sons should not be punished for the sins of the fathers (2 Kgs 14:6), but this is not the principle at work here. It is one thing for a son or successor to be absolved of blame for the sin of a father, but it is quite another thing when the son and his successors deliberately choose to imitate the actions of the father. Jeroboam was an apostate, and none of the successive Israelite kings chose to alter this course. Some, like Omri and Ahab, chose to further the apostasy and are condemned as being the worst kings ever (1 Kgs 16:25, 30-34). This brings them into serious confrontation with the spokesmen of God, Elijah and Elisha. The judgment of the writer of Kings is that *no king in Israel ever attained the ideal.* In the words of another biblical writer, and in another context, "all have sinned and fall short of the glory of God" (Rom 3:23).

With the nation of Judah, matters are a little more complicated. Of the twenty monarchs after Solomon, including Athaliah the usurper (2 Kgs 11), eight are accounted as good. They are Asa (1 Kgs 15:14), Jehoshaphat (1 Kgs 22:43), Jehoash

(2 Kgs 12:2), Amaziah, with qualifications 2 Kgs 14:3, 4), Azariah (2 Kgs 15:3), Jotham (2 Kgs 15:34), Hezekiah (2 Kgs 18:3), and Josiah (2 Kgs 22:2). The standard of behavior is set by David, whose heart was faithful to God. Some, like Hezekiah and especially Josiah, were very faithful. Of the twelve remaining, Athaliah is not evaluated, probably because she was not a "legitimate" monarch of the southern kingdom. Note that there is no formal introduction or dismissal of her reign. The eleven left are all judged as apostate. They either follow the ways of Rehoboam, or imitate the kings of Israel. Six are compared to Manasseh, either directly or by implication. The strongest condemnation of all is reserved for Manasseh himself. Of him it is said that he "behaved . . . according to the disgusting actions of the nations whom Yahweh had driven out before the Israelites." (2 Kgs 21:2 WBC). The accusation is telling on two counts. First, it shows that in the author's mind, the standard of behavior is the deuteronomic law (see Deut 18:9–14). And, second, it is the most damning of all accusations because it shows that Manasseh acted as though the giving of the land —a promise of the Exodus and Sinai covenant according to Deuteronomy—had never taken place. He, like Ahab, chose to live "before the covenant." In Judah, there is a mixture of obedience and disobedience, of faithfulness and apostasy.

It is tempting to view these judgments of the deuteronomist's in a way that makes his theological evaluation of the two nations, Israel and Judah, sound mechanical. They had sinned, therefore they were punished. But he does not mistreat his sources by forcing them into this rigid scheme. He is aware that the history of a nation is never so neat and tidy. There are aberrations, differences, and ambiguities which must be accommodated. In fact, in his treatment of the kings of Israel and Judah, there are surprises.

One of the blessings of keeping the covenant is "length of days," or long life. Conversely, disobedience leads to being "cut off." However, the apostate king Ahab, who is most strongly condemned for his sins, reigned a total of twenty-two years (1 Kgs 16:29–22:40). Jehu reigned for twenty-eight years (2 Kgs 9:1–10:36), Jeroboam II reigned for forty-one years (2 Kgs 14:23–29), and Manasseh for an impressive fifty-five years (2 Kgs 21:1–18). In fact, of the twenty-seven "bad" kings of Israel and Judah, one (Manasseh) reigned for over fifty years, one (Jeroboam II) reigned for over forty years, five reigned for over twenty years, and eight for more than ten years. There seems to be no hard and fast correlation between faithfulness and length of reign.

Nor are material prosperity and territorial expansion restricted to "good" kings either. In fact, after David and Solomon, the two kingdoms see their greatest expansion (2 Kgs 14:25) during the reigns of Jeroboam II in the north (a bad king) and his contemporary Uzziah in the south (a good but leprous king). The most significant losses in the south happened during the reigns of the good kings Hezekiah and Josiah.

Another interesting treatment by the author is of those kings generally regarded as good. They include Asa, Jehoshaphat, Jehoash, Amaziah (qualified), Azariah, Jotham, Hezekiah, and Josiah—all of Judah.

The fate of most of these is anomalous. Asa dies with a disease of the feet (1 Kgs 15:23) which some believe may have been gout (disfigurement had a strong negative symbolic meaning in the Bible). Jehoash of Judah was not only a good king, restorer of the Davidic dynasty, but also a reformer of the temple. He died prematurely, assassinated by his own people in Jerusalem (2 Kgs 12:19–21). Amaziah also was assassinated (2 Kgs 14:17–22). Azariah (Uzziah) died a leper (2 Kgs 15:5). Hezekiah's kingdom suffered invasion and he himself—another great reformer—suffered from skin disease (2 Kgs 20:1–11). Finally, Josiah, the greatest reformer, died prematurely at the hands of an invading foreign king (2 Kgs 23:28-30).

What is the significance then of the anomalous fates of the good and bad kings of Israel and Judah? First, it is clear that the writer offers a much more complex interpretation of the history than a simplistic "sin and judgment" model. He takes sin seriously, and he takes the judgment of the Exile seriously; but he interprets the history from a fuller perspective. On the one hand are the kings of Israel and Judah, acting as though they were free, making their own choices (frequently the wrong ones); and on the other hand is God, truly acting as a free agent. From the beginning, under the leadership of her kings, the nation of Israel as a whole has chosen to live in apostasy and under judgment. This is established very clearly in the record of the reign of Jeroboam ben Nebat (1 Kgs 12, 13). There are temporary delays of the judgment and occasional enlargements of territory and growth in prosperity, but these do not prevent the eventual judgment. They happen because of God's grace and mercy (2 Kgs 13:5, 22; 14:25-27).

Many of the kings of Judah behaved "in the ways of the kings of Israel." Here and in prophetic literature (e.g., Jer 3, 4) the implication is that Judah can therefore expect the same consequences (2 Kgs 17:19). Thus it is that "good" kings can do nothing to halt the inevitable move toward judgment. Their deformities, sicknesses, and untimely deaths cast a long shadow on Judah's history as well. The delay in judgment for Judah is not due to any human action, but "for my own sake and for the sake of my servant David" (1 Kgs 11:11-13; 2 Kgs 19:34; 20:5-6). Thus a picture is drawn, as Ellul points out, of kings and humans acting in seeming independence—yet with each act further enslaving them—and of God acting in freedom, bound only by his word and his honor.

The nature of prophecy in Israel

Prophets are no strangers to readers of the Old Testament. In the traditional Jewish reckoning, prophetic material makes up one third of the Hebrew Bible—the Tanak, a word coined from the initial letters of the Hebrew words for "Law" (Torah), "Prophets" (Nebi'im), and "Writings" (Kethubim).

The prophets appear on its pages as men and women who declared the Word of God for specific human situations. They had a special relationship with God which gave them peculiar insight into the nature of historical situations (an insight which was often at odds with the generally accepted view of things), and unique understanding of the nature and will of God. The best way of conveying the essence of prophecy is to let one of them speak for himself (italics are mine).

> But as for me, I am filled with power,
>   with the Spirit of the LORD,
>   and with justice and might,

to declare to Jacob his transgression
and to Israel his sin. (Mic 3:8)

The historical origins of prophecy are obscure, and a variety of people in the early days of Israel's life in Canaan were called prophets—for example, Deborah and Samuel, who were both otherwise known as judges. Gideon's call to defeat the Midianites (Judg 6) is remarkably similar to the call of Jeremiah (Jer 1:4–10), but he too was better known as a judge. What emerges in the prophetic tradition, as Israel's history develops, is the consciousness that the prophets have of standing in a great tradition of speakers for God, a tradition that began with the prophet par excellence, Moses.

This is especially true in Deuteronomy and the deuteronomistic history. In Deuteronomy 18:18 the perpetuation of a Mosaic prophetic tradition is promised, and many of the subsequent prophets follow in Moses' footsteps. These footsteps follow the path of the covenant between God and his people. Like Moses, many of the prophets act as negotiators between the two partners, praying for the people on the one hand, but declaring the Word of God without compromise on the other.

The covenant involved an exclusive worship of the God of Israel who rescued her from Egypt. This is a theme which echoes again and again in the literature of the prophets. Like Elijah, the true prophet is jealous for the Lord. But beyond this, the covenant involved a moral imperative of mutual caring and support among the people of God. Each member of the covenant community was special and was to be cared for by others. Finally, the covenant involved an absolute dependence upon God for help, deliverance, and sustenance. These ideas form the framework from which the prophets operated.

Another interesting feature about the prophetic tradition is that it became most vocal during the time of the monarchy. The prophets became the watchdogs of the monarchy. This link between prophet and king became so strong that when the monarchy disappeared during the Exile, Jewish tradition maintained that prophecy also ceased—to be revived again only at the coming of the Messiah, a point well appreciated by the writer of Acts (see especially Peter's speech in Acts 2:14–40).

Like Moses, many prophets found themselves to be critics of the status quo, especially when what passed for the status quo was detrimental to the covenant ideals. It was often the case that this status quo was established and maintained by the king. The prophets' attitude of confrontation with established power gave rise to the uncompromising nature of biblical prophecy. Each prophet speaks with the unshakable conviction that the Word of God is to be listened to and obeyed. There are no half measures. Two ways are set out, one leading to life, the other to death. The people must choose. To refuse to choose is to opt for death (1 Kgs 18:21). The language of the biblical prophets is therefore strong and forceful. It is often full of hyperbole, as the passion of the prophet for the Word of God and the well-being of the audience takes over. At times it is almost as though language is inadequate to express what is in the mind of the prophet. "Fire in the bones" is experienced, but how does one give voice to it?

Because of the nature of the task the prophets were given, and because of the nature of the circumstances into which they were thrust, the prophet's involvement in the task was absolute. Prophecy allowed for no compromise, and as a result the personal lives of the prophets were deeply affected. Few were married—and to never marry was unusual in ancient Israel. Many were alone and rejected, and many were persecuted. They lived for the Word of God, which they received through visions, through dreams, through understanding and reflection—which they then passed on to the people. They were, in the words of one of their number, watchmen, burdened with a heavy responsibility, which was not for the weak.

Prophets and kings

Prophets abound in Kings. That faithful friend and advisor to David, the prophet Nathan, was active in the struggle for the succession, and he took part in the anointing of the new king, Solomon. In 1 Kings 11:11-13 Solomon is addressed by God, presumably through a prophet, concerning his apostasy. It was by a prophet, Ahijah of Shiloh, that God announced to Jeroboam that the kingdom would be split after the death of Solomon (1 Kgs 11:29-39). When the northern nation seceded, and the southern king Rehoboam wanted to force them back into a united kingdom through war, it was a prophet, Shemaiah, who thwarted this move (1 Kgs 12:22-24).

An anonymous "man of God" (one of the terms for a prophet) prophesied against Israel and foretold the rise of Josiah (1 Kgs 13:1-10). But as that chapter shows, even the prophet himself was subject to the Word of God; he died because of disobedience. Ahijah of Shiloh reappears in 1 Kings 14:2-15. He cannot be tricked by Jeroboam, and he announces the coming demise of the dynasty of Jeroboam, and raises the possibility of a future exile of Israel.

Lesser-known prophets appear in the narrative, such as Jehu ben Hananiah who foretold the destruction of the house of Baasha (1 Kgs 16:1-4). Even Joshua ben Nun was given prophetic status (1 Kgs 16:34) when Hiel restored Jericho. During the activities of Elijah, at least one hundred faithful prophets were persecuted by Jezebel (1 Kgs 18:4). From 1 Kings 20:13-15 we learn that one part of a prophet's role was advice in warfare. Later in the same chapter (vv 35-43) another anonymous prophet appears before the king on a matter of foreign policy—how to treat a captured enemy king. These roles are found again in 1 Kings 22:1-28 as the majority of court prophets advise in favor of the campaign against Ramoth Gilead, and find in their midst one dissenting voice (vv 13-23), that of Micaiah ben Imlah.

Other prophets appear in the narrative, such as Jonah ben Amittai (2 Kgs 14:25) and Isaiah of Jerusalem (2 Kgs 19:1-20:19). Huldah the prophetess (2 Kgs 22:14) advises Josiah on the content and meaning of the book of Torah found during his repairs of the temple. Anonymous prophets (2 Kgs 21:10-15) condemn the reign of Manasseh for its wickedness and corruption. Finally, when the writer of 1 and 2 Kings wishes to summarize the moral condition of the people and their kings, he turns to general prophetic statements which capture his meaning well (2 Kgs 17:13, 23; 23:27; 24:2-4).

In addition to knowing and using the royal archives, the writer of Kings must have had access to countless stories of prophets throughout the history of Israel and Judah which had been preserved by the faithful followers and supporters of the prophets. Taking these with the stories of the kings and the political fortunes and misfortunes of the kings and prophets, our writer weaves an historical narrative which sees things clearly *sub specie aeternitatis*. It is history, but history interpreted according to the will of God in that history. It is a powerful exposition of the statement made by Amos of Tekoa that "surely the Lord does nothing without revealing his secret to his servants the prophets" (Amos 3:7).

Prophets and politics

When one surveys the role of the prophets in 1 and 2 Kings, the question of the prophets' relationship to political life inevitably arises. In our minds so much of what prophets do in these narratives can come under a political label rather than a religious one. But we have to remember that this kind of distinction between religious and political, or sacred and

31

secular, is our distinction, one that would not have been recognized by the ancient Israelite. In the ancient Near East in general, and in ancient Israel and Judah in particular, all of life was seen as having some connection with religion or religious ideology. The nature of "politics" for Israel consisted in the acknowledgement of a group identity: one people (Israel), one God (Yahweh), and obedience to the covenant instructions which bound them together. It would be impossible, for example, to go through the law-codes of the Old Testament and to separate out the "religious" from the "secular." All law presupposes the existence and identity of Israel's God, Yahweh, as the deliverer from Egypt.

Israel's identity as a people is to be seen only in relationship to her God. She is the "bride" of Yahweh (Hos 1–3, Jer 2:1–10), the "son" of Yahweh (Hos 11:1), his "special people," his "heritage." Israel does not have an identity apart from God. Therefore, members of this community live their lives in light of this relationship with God. Nothing—whether it be agriculture, family life, neighborly relations, warfare, or government—can be seen apart from God. Deuteronomy makes this very plain, and this concept is carried into the deuteronomistic history.

It is understandable that the prophets' speaking out (on behalf of God) on matters of national policy appears political from our point of view. But every aspect of Israel's life was seen by them as being under the judgment of God. Nathan's involvement in the succession intrigue as the death of David approached is to be seen not just as political, but also as connected to God's promise to David in 2 Samuel 7. The involvement of Ahijah and Shemaiah in the split of the kingdoms is indeed involvement in political activity (1 Kgs 11:29ff; 12:22ff), but it has a religious and moral dimension as well—these events are a judgment of God on the people. In fact, all the prophetic pronouncements in 1 and 2 Kings relate to the political life of the people, since the political life is the arena in which the ideology (covenant) is to be worked out in practice. Therefore, apostasy has political as well as religious consequences. As other prophets were to expound, mistreatment of one's own people, especially the poor and marginalized, is not only a social scandal, but a religious sin.

Prophets and history

According to the deuteronomistic history, the role of the prophet is not simply one of meddling in the political life of the people. The role of the prophet is far more important and one might say, awe-inspiring, because the prophet and the Word of God he or she utters is at the heart of the meaning of history. As Gerhard von Rad put it:

> There . . . exists . . . an inter-relationship between the words of Jahweh and history in the sense that Jahweh's word, once uttered, reaches its goal under all circumstances in history.[1]

This is not a magical relationship between word and historical action, nor is it a relationship caused by what von Rad called "the power inherent in" the word. For the deuteronomist, history makes sense only as the fulfillment of God's Word. The history of Israel and Judah, from the perspective of the deuteronomist and his contemporaries, had ended in disaster, the Exile. How was this to be understood? Was it the result of an abandonment by God? Or was there some other purpose to it all? The deuteronomist presents it as the inevitable conclusion to the action of the Word of God in history.

One way of developing this theme was by showing that major events in the life and history of Israel and Judah were not merely fortuitous, nor the result of capriciousness on

33

the part of God, but given purpose by the Word of God. Von Rad has done a great service by listing the eleven "promise-fulfillment" texts in 1 and 2 Kings.

Promise	Fulfillment
2 Sam 7:13	1 Kgs 8:20
1 Kgs 11:29–39	1 Kgs 12:15b
1 Kgs 13	2 Kgs 23:16–18
1 Kgs 14:6–16	1 Kgs 15:29
1 Kgs 16:1–4	1 Kgs 16:12
Josh 6:26	1 Kgs 16:34
1 Kgs 22:17	1 Kgs 22:35–40
1 Kgs 21:21–23	1 Kgs 21:27–29
2 Kgs 1:6	2 Kgs 1:17
2 Kgs 21:10–15	2 Kgs 24:2
2 Kgs 22:15–20	2 Kgs 23:30^2

The history of Israel and Judah are not so much controlled as given meaning, and that meaning comes by the Word of God given through the prophets. As we have seen, there is freedom for men and women to act within this history, but ultimately, there is no escape from moral responsibility. God's Word continually interrupts human activity to evaluate and to pass judgment. Nowhere is this more clear in 1 and 2 Kings than in the stories associated with the personalities and actions of the two great prophets Elijah and Elisha.

Elijah and Elisha

Elijah and Elisha deserve separate treatment. Almost one-third of the material in 1 and 2 Kings is devoted to their activities. They step onto the stage of Israelite history at a time of crisis. Omri had established a firm hold on the northern kingdom, and his son Ahab consolidated that hold in a way similar to Solomon's—by an extensive building program and by alliances with neighboring countries. Ahab married Jezebel, daughter of the king of Tyre and, by all accounts, became controlled by this woman of very strong character. For Israel's worship of Yahweh, the alliance between Ahab and Jezebel was a disaster. Baalism was established throughout the country, and open conflict broke out between the agents of Jezebel and the worshipers of Yahweh. Ahab acquiesced in this policy, and the worship of Yahweh—the God who had rescued Israel from Egypt—was in danger of extinction. It is into this setting that Elijah comes.

1 Kings 17–2 Kings 2 is taken up with stories of Elijah, almost without a break, and 2 Kings 2–13 covers the ministry of Elisha, with a brief detour into the activities of Elisha's protégé, Jehu, in chapters 9 and 10 and a look at the events in the south in chapters 11 and 12. These stories, which are quite varied in form and purpose, were undoubtedly taken from a corpus of stories about these prophets collected by their supporters and followers, the "sons of the prophets." There are some slight differences in the presentation of the stories connected with each prophet. The Elijah stories tend to be longer, and in their present form each story takes up a chapter, whereas the Elisha stories move from theme to theme quite quickly. (In the WBC 12, 13, attention is paid to the literary presentation of these stories and their narrative and plot development, and that material does not need repeating here.) A significant feature of both collections of stories is that Elijah and Elisha are presented as very human characters, both of whom have doubts and disappointments in their ministries.

The relationship of the two prophets is fascinating. At one point Elisha is referred to as the one "who poured water on the hands of Elijah" (2 Kgs 3:11), and at another point as one who "ministered to" Elijah (1 Kgs 19:21). Both of these references point to a close relationship of master and servant or teacher and disciple, although little of this is given any form in the rest of the stories. This close relationship is reflected in the story of the departure of Elijah in 2 Kings 2, when Elisha alone is allowed to cross the Jordan and witness the departure, whereas the other followers, the "sons of the prophets," stand at a distance.

Elijah makes his appearance in the Old Testament in a very abrupt manner in 1 Kings 17:1. This might well be for literary effect, but it also indicates that the original readers were probably familiar with the man, and for them he needed no introduction. Although the "sons of the prophets" are mentioned in the collection of Elijah stories (1 Kgs 20:35–43), it is not in direct association with Elijah. These supporters of the prophets (see WBC 13:25–27) were obviously active during Elijah's time, but it was during the ministry of Elisha that the connections are most closely seen. It is quite possible that Elisha was originally an "outsider" to this group. His appointing in 1 Kings 19:19–21, and the story of his succession in 2 Kings 2:1–18, appear as if they might be making a strong case for Elisha's assumption of the mantle of Elijah against some opposition from the group itself.

Whatever the precise relationship, it is clear that a third figure, who binds the two together, is Moses. The story of Elijah's departure in 2 Kings 2:1–18 has too many allusions to events in the life of Moses and Joshua for it to be accidental. The precise point of the Jordan crossing is the same, the actions are the same, and, like Moses, Elijah has no visible grave. Elisha becomes Elijah's Joshua, commissioned to carry on the prophetic task on this side of the Jordan. God had not left himself without witness (cf. Acts 14:17) at this, a crucial time in the history of Israel—the years following the death of the apostate Ahab (2 Kgs 1:1). The question that arises is, can things improve, or will they get worse? Elisha the prophet offers answers to this question.

If we move back to the stories of Elijah and examine them, several well-worn prophetic themes emerge. In the first stories of the widow in Zarephath (1 Kgs 17:8-16, 17-24), the dominant theme is *reciprocal compassion*. In a time of famine, Elijah has been provided for by God (1 Kgs 17:1-7) until the food is exhausted. He is then sent to Zarephath, in Gentile territory, where a widow has been chosen to provide for him. Her complaints quickly give way to willingness to assist the prophet of God, and she and her son are provided for as well. In the story of the death and revival of the widow's son (1 Kgs 17:17-24) a similar compassion is shown. Through prayer Elijah restores the son to his mother.

In 1 Kings 18, the issue is *exclusive worship of Yahweh*, a matter over which conflict had broken out between Jezebel's supporters and the worshipers of Yahweh. It was a question of the very survival of the name and reputation of Yahweh in the north. If Jezebel had her way, the northern kingdom would lose its distinctiveness and its identity as a partner in the covenant with God. No more serious question could be faced by a prophet of God. The Carmel confrontation demonstrates the absolute incomparability of Yahweh. And Elijah's mocking of the prophets of Baal (1 Kgs 18:25-29) anticipates the similar derision of false gods by the great prophet of the Exile (Isa 44:9-20), and echoes the wonder expressed in Deuteronomy 4:6-7, 32-40, at the uniqueness of Israel and her experience with God. On these matters the prophet will brook no compromise.

The next chapter, 1 Kings 19, deals with the matter of the *prophetic task*. Here, Elijah is disillusioned and obviously somewhat depressed. His vision is blurred by his self-centeredness. He retreats eventually to Horeb, wishing to die. God's response is simple. Elijah is to stand once again where Moses stood. He is, in effect, recommissioned. So Elijah returns to continue his work—to raise up kings, to appoint a successor, and to continue to champion the cause of the covenant. Elijah's whole being was subject to this commission.

The best-known story of Elijah concerns Naboth's vineyard, and Ahab and Jezebel's cowardly maneuvers to wrest it from him (1 Kgs 21). The issue here is *justice*, based on the covenant. The divisions of the land of promise in Joshua 13–18 are based on the notion that the land is a gift from God (see ch 5 below). Each tribe and each tribal member is granted a place in that promise; therefore, it is a sin to remove a neighbor's landmark (Deut 19:14; 27:17), and a disruption of the covenant to take someone else's land. Thus it is that when Elijah confronts Ahab on the matter, he uses very specific language, "Have you killed, and also taken possession?" (1 Kgs 21:19). It is the language of the Decalogue, which forbids both murder (Deut 5:17) and the coveting of a neighbor's field (Deut 5:21).

Each of these themes is repeated in one form or another in the stories of Elisha. Elisha, too, shows compassion to those in need (2 Kgs 4:1–4); is jealous for the exclusive worship of Yahweh (2 Kgs 3:13, 14); experiences doubts and despair over his prophetic task (2 Kgs 6:32, 33); and is concerned with matters of justice (2 Kgs 8:7–15). The deuteronomic law commanded care for the powerless in society—the widow, the orphan, and the stranger (Deut 14:29; 16:11, 14). And it is precisely these people who experience the care and compassion of the two great prophets Elijah and Elisha.

Apart from these two prophets, so powerfully portrayed in these stories, several other characters stand out. As one might expect, however, the kings and their courtiers are rarely shown in a sympathetic light. Ahab is the arch apostate who finds a worthy opponent in Elijah. Ahaziah's claim to fame is a fall down some stairs, an illness, and a search for healing in a foreign country (2 Kgs 1). The two kings in 2 Kings 3 panic when they find themselves lost in the desert (2 Kgs 3:10). The kings of Israel and Syria misinterpret the need of Naaman, and almost begin a war over the issue of his visit to Elisha (2 Kgs 5:1–7). Court officials fare no better. The pompous arrogance of the captain's disbelieving reaction to Elisha's prophecy in 2 Kings 7:1, 2 results in his untimely death (2 Kgs 7:16–20).

On the other hand, it is frequently the lesser known and the unimportant who become agents of healing, restoration, and fulfillment. In 2 Kings 3:11 it is a servant of the king of Israel who guides the panic-stricken kings to seek out Elisha. In 2 Kings 5:2, 3 it is a young Hebrew slave-girl who begins the process of Naaman's healing. In 2 Kings 7 it is the unlikely quartet of outcast lepers who discover that the Syrian army besieging Samaria has fled and who carry the good news to the king. Even Gehazi, the discredited servant of Elisha, helps in the restoration of the Shunemite's land when she returns from exile (2 Kgs 8:5). There is a wonderful principle at work here. Paul captured it well in his first letter to Corinth.

> For consider your call . . . not many of you were wise according to worldly standards, not many were powerful, not many were of noble birth; but God chose what is foolish in the world to shame the wise, God chose what is weak in the world to shame the strong, God chose what is low and despised in the world, even things that are not, to bring to nothing things that are. . . . (1 Cor 1:26–28)

Jesus himself chose the "ignorant and unlearned" to follow him. He associated with tax collectors, and accepted those whom others deemed unacceptable.

In Elijah and Elisha, Israel knew that "there was a prophet in Israel," and that "there was a God in Israel." This is a theme repeated many times in the narratives (1 Kgs 17:24; 2 Kgs 1:3, 16; 3:11; 4:9; 5:2, 3), and recognized more often by foreigners than by Israelites! Elijah earned the reputation of a "troubler of Israel" (1 Kgs 18:17) and Elisha earned the respect of kings (2 Kgs 8:7-10; 13:14), but they had in common the heart and soul of prophecy: the uncompromising championship of the Word of God in human affairs. In George Mendenhall's words,

> they had a vision of a Transcendent deity whose governance over the historical process made inevitable the destruction of a petty political power that regarded the deity as a mere security blanket with which to cover up . . . oppression and corruption.[3]

4 THE PEOPLE OF GOD

In 1 and 2 Kings, monarchs reign over and lead their people, but are themselves under a higher law. Alongside them, prophets proclaim that higher law with their utterances of the divine Word. They stand as guardians of society, proclaiming the will of the covenant God, Yahweh, and playing an intermediary role between the people and God. Thus, both kings and prophets represent forms of leadership. A third form of leadership is that of the priest, who, while not absent from 1 and 2 Kings, is certainly not very prominent. But what of the people, who are led by both king and prophet? How are they understood in Kings?

The nature of God's people

The writer of 1 and 2 Kings would have had a considerable knowledge of the history of the people of Israel and Judah, and of the early literature of the people. The history of Abraham, Isaac, and Jacob, the ancestors of Israel whose stories are recorded in sections of Genesis, would have been familiar to him in some form, and he acknowledges the covenant with the patriarchs (2 Kgs 13:23; 17:15). The traditions about the slavery in Egypt, the Exodus, the wilderness wanderings, and the covenant at Sinai are all clearly known and cited by him (2 Kgs 17:7-18). Further, the role of Moses, the architect of the newly-freed society, was also part of his knowledge. These facts are crucial elements in the formation of the notion of the "people of God." They are foundational to Israel's self-understanding, and part of the personal and public history of the writer.

We ought also to guard against reading too many modern, Western concepts into the term "people." Unfortunately this occurs all too often in Old Testament studies, but we cannot stress enough some of the differences in meaning between a biblical (i.e., ancient Mediterranean) understanding of "people" and a modern North American understanding. Biblical terms like "people of Israel" carry with them quite different sets of meaning than terms like "people of Canada" or "the American people." The latter terms encompass a variety of different ethnic backgrounds and languages, something that would have been unthinkable in the ancient Near East. For us, binding forces are mainly symbolic, like the flag, the country, or a political ideology. In the biblical world, the binding force was kinship—real or supposed. All came from one father, Abraham, and all were therefore related. In the Bible this is seen most clearly in the stories of the twelve sons of Jacob/Israel, who become tribal heads. Even though the sociopolitical form of the people of God underwent several far-reaching changes throughout biblical history—from tribal clan, to tribal league, to monarchy, to priestly theocracy—it never lost this sense of belonging. This sense of group identity was always very strong, so much so, that even at the end of the biblical period of their history, this people is still known as "Israel" (Mal 1:1).

The outward form that this people took prior to the monarchy was that of a theocracy; they were a people ruled by God and his Law. This Law was given to Moses at Sinai and formed the basis of the community after Sinai. In Joshua and Judges, the Law is presupposed as foundational to the life and well-being of the people. A glance at these books will show that kinship predominated the people's self-understanding. What political life existed was dominated by males, and political decisions were made almost exclusively by male elders. Even in those relatively early days, priests, prophets, and judges shared various combined religious, civil, and military powers among them—as is seen in the careers of Deborah, Gideon, Samuel, and, of course, Moses. Many decisions were made at the local, that is village and town level. The story of Ruth offers a good example of this.

As we have seen, a decisive shift comes with the advent of monarchy, and our writer is fully aware of the nature of this shift. He understands well the nature of monarchical society. In this society there was a lessening of the power and influence of the elders (1 Kgs 12:6–11), and a concomitant growth in the power of the newly created center of society, the king's court (2 Sam 8:15; 1 Kgs 4:1–6). Decisions that will affect the entire population of Israel are now made by a small group, and an impersonal administration is empowered to carry out those decisions. Tasks are shared among a different set of people, some known, some unknown, and some even non-Israelite. Dominating the whole scene is the political will of the central figure, the king. In such circumstances, the fate and well-being of the people of God assumes a new importance. God, of course, remains faithful, but the loyalty and faithfulness of the people is now put to new tests.

For the modern reader, the use of "Israel" (the older term for the people of God) in 1 and 2 Kings may cause some confusion, stemming from the fact that the term now has a broader meaning, while still retaining some of the old. It is clear that the term is applied to the populace of the tribes, then under control of the monarchy. Solomon, after his victory in the civil war following the death of David, becomes king over "all Israel" (1 Kgs 4:1), that is, the territory left to him by David. The same meaning is implied in the use of "Israel" in 1 Kings 6:1, and possibly 8:1. Elsewhere, this territory is also called "the kingdom" (1 Kgs 11:31).

In other passages, however, a clear distinction is made between Judah, the southern kingdom following the split after Solomon's death, and Israel, the northern kingdom consisting of ten tribes. Thus in 1 Kings 1:35 and 4:35, the phrase "Israel and Judah" applies to what previously was referred to as "all Israel." The distinction is maintained in 1 Kings 13 in the story of the man of God from Judah and the prophet from Israel. In the same vein, Jeroboam's appeal to the northern tribes to reject Rehoboam's attitude and rule is prefaced with the phrase "O Israel!" (1 Kgs 12:16). Further, the phrase "my people Israel," which is used in 2 Samuel 7:8 of the entire covenant community, is used in 1 Kings 16:2 exclusively of the northern kingdom.

Yet there persists throughout 1 and 2 Kings an understanding of "Israel" as referring to all the recipients of God's grace at the Exodus, as hearers of his Law at Sinai, and partners in the covenant with him. Thus when Solomon is made king, he asks for an understanding mind to govern "thy great people" (1 Kgs 3:9; see also 8:41). When the kingdom is split, it is the result of Solomon's disobedience to a law which God gave to "the people of Israel" (1 Kgs 11:2, see Deut 17:17), and by way of contrast, Hezekiah removed from the temple the bronze cult object which "the people of Israel" had revered since the time of Moses (2 Kgs 18:4).

Finally, when kings of either the north or south are addressed in prophetic terms in 1 and 2 Kings, they are addressed by the "God of Israel" (in other words, the God of Sinai and of the covenant). It is this God who announces through the prophet Elijah that a drought will come on the northern nation of Israel (1 Kgs 17:1), but it is also this same God who announces to Josiah through Huldah the prophetess the consequences of the breaking of the covenant (2 Kgs 22:15).

There is, then, some ambiguity in the terminology used to refer to the people, but no discontinuity. Ultimately, for the writer of the history of the monarchy, all the people of God are bound by the covenant to the same God regardless of whether they are known as "Israel" or "Judah." This position is basic to the prophetic tradition, which had to face the same ambiguity. At times, the northern nation of Israel is addressed (Hos 4:1; 5:1) and, at times, the southern nation of Judah is (Jer 4:3). On occasion, the ambiguity is lessened by the use of specific references to places such as Samaria or Jerusalem (Mic 1:5), but on other occasions the ambiguity remains. However, the continuity remains also, no matter what the outward political form of the people.

Responsibility

Although the fundamental concept of the people of God applies to Israel in one form or another throughout the Old Testament, the shift in political structure from tribal to monarchical does have an effect on one aspect of Israel's existence. In the period of the judges, responsibility for Israel's disobedience and apostasy rests entirely with the people. It is consistently "the people of Israel" who "did what was evil in the sight of the Lord" (e.g., Judg 2:11; 3:7, 12; 4:1; 6:1).

In the period of the monarchy, our writer makes plain time and again that it is now the monarchs who "did what was evil in the sight of the Lord" (e.g., 1 Kgs 15:26, 34). In so doing, the kings followed in the ways of the archapostate Jeroboam, and "made Israel to sin" (1 Kgs 15:25, 26). Increased power of leadership involved increased responsibility to lead properly. It is this point which is taken up by some of the prophets, such as Jeremiah, who are placed in opposition to the leaders of Israel and Judah (Jer 1:18, 19; Mic 3:1, 9).

But good leadership, in part, is dependent upon a willingness to be led well, and the new system in no way absolves the people of their own responsibility to worship and fear Yahweh. Shepherds have an enormous responsibility for those whom God has given into their charge, and numerous prophetic voices have been raised to make this point (Jer 19–23; Ezek 34). But ultimately it is the lament of the prophet that "my people have .   forsaken me, the fountain of living waters, and hewed out cisterns for themselves, broken cisterns, that can hold no water" (Jer 2:13). Being in the tradition of the prophetic outlook on human affairs, our writer is fully aware of this (see 1 Kgs 14:21, 22).

People and covenant

In the Old Testament as a whole, and certainly in the understanding of our writer, the basis for the relationship between God and his people, and the justification for God's claim to their obedience and reverence, is the covenant (berith). No other concept has dominated the discussion on the Old Testament more than the covenant, and the attention is well-deserved. It is a central topic, of great importance to the understanding of the nature of the people of God in 1 and 2 Kings and elsewhere.

To describe the notion of covenant as "a formal agreement or treaty between two parties, with each assuming some obligation" is correct, but only partly so. Although many parallels have been found in the political world of the ancient Near East, the concept cannot be confined to the world of politics, particularly politics as we understand it. Strictly speaking, a covenant is not a business contract, although trading partners form "covenants" with each other to further trade. Some scholars have emphasized the element of obligation laid upon the partners in a covenant; but again, it is this, and more than this. Other kinds of agreements are encompassed by the term, such as the agreement between two close friends, David and Jonathan (1 Sam 18:3), which certainly transcends any concept of a formal contract.

Interpreters have long been aware of the many parallels between the Old Testament idea of covenant and the numerous treaties drawn up between nations of the ancient Near East. Some of the treaty texts date from as early as the fifteenth century B.C., and as late as the seventh. They span much of the history of Israel in Old Testament times. So much of the language and form is the same that it appears that Old Testament writers and leaders saw the covenant concept as a perfect illustration of the relationship of God to his people. There is nothing unusual in this; other biblical writers have taken institutions of daily life in the biblical world and used them as illustrations of spiritual concepts. The language of salvation is the language of warfare and slavery. God is likened to a warrior or a father, and the people of God are regarded as a family. If the international treaty was so widespread, then it would have provided an excellent aid to understanding Israel's relationship to God.

International treaties have been classified into two types: the *parity* treaty, an agreement between (more or less) equals; and the *suzerainty* treaty, an agreement between a conquering overlord and a vassal. The unequal relationship between God and Israel is well-illustrated by this latter form, and the book of Deuteronomy shows a remarkably close affinity to the pattern and language of the known suzerainty treaty texts.

Yet if we understand the analogy only as a formal political one, we have not fully understood the nature of the relationship between God and Israel. Aside from the fact that illustrations tend to be incomplete, they must be understood properly. Although the treaty texts are from the realm of international politics, we must not view that realm as though it were a duplicate of modern politics. We need to see it in the social and cultural context of the ancient Near East, especially in light of the way relationships were perceived and how they functioned.

From the perspective of our individualistic way of perceiving and living our lives, it is difficult for us to understand that in the ancient (and modern) Mediterranean world, relationships had a much stronger element of dependence, especially dependence upon persons with power. As one writer has recently expressed it, "Ideal superiors are benevolent autocrats or paternalists, good 'fathers' on whom subordinates like to depend." The relationship between suzerain and vassal is not so much that between "boss and underling," as between "patron and client," with mutual dependence being a prominent element of the bond between the two. The vassal/client is dependent on the suzerain/patron for protection and status; in turn, the patron is dependent upon the client for respect and honor.

To a large extent it is the "good name" of the patron that the client is responsible for in keeping his side of the relationship. Thus it is that the suzerain/patron always presents himself in an extended, self-serving introduction in the treaty texts. Thus it is too, that God prefaces the Decalogue with a self-presentation claiming honor and exclusive worship.

This understanding of the relationship between partners of a covenant is also seen in another model from the ancient

Near East, the "covenant of grant," a gift of land and status to a client king by a god. This form is thought to offer some insight into the background to the covenant with David.

This rather lengthy diversion into the notion of covenant is important as background to its use in 1 and 2 Kings. It stresses the element of the personal relationship between the two partners, an element which tends to get lost if the covenant is seen only in rather cold political terms.

In 1 and 2 Kings the term "covenant" is applied to a number of situations. The trade agreement between Solomon and Hiram of Tyre (1 Kgs 5:26 [5:12]) and the agreement bringing an end to war between Israel and Syria (1 Kgs 15:19; 20:34), are called "covenants," and would probably have been formalized in the same way that many parity and suzerainty treaties were. When Jehoiada the priest conspires to overthrow the usurper queen Athaliah, he allies himself with the palace guard in a "covenant" (2 Kgs 11:4). When the revolt is over, God, king, and people are reunited in a "covenant" (2 Kgs 11:17) reminiscent of the agreement between David and the northern tribes (2 Sam 5:3) and the agreement between Rehoboam and the northern tribes left in tatters by Solomon (1 Kgs 12:6–16).

Basic to Israel's understanding of her status before God is the agreement made between God and Israel's ancestors Abraham, Isaac, and Jacob. Reminiscent of the "covenant of grant," its strongest element is the notion of "gift." It represents an act of grace, of munificence. It is recalled as such in 2 Kings 13:23, and its rejection is lamented in 2 Kings 17:15. Its twin is the covenant made between God and Israel at Sinai, when the Torah was given to order the life of the covenant people.

Because of the nature of these books as part of the deuteronomistic history, it is no surprise to see this covenant referred to again and again in 1 and 2 Kings. Its most important symbol, the ark of the covenant, is at the very center of

Israel's life, in its most sacred place, the Holy of Holies (1 Kgs 6:19; 8:1–21). Centuries later, Josiah's workmen rediscovered the covenant Torah, and he attempted to restore the covenant to its rightful place in the life of God's people (2 Kgs 23:2–21).

The tragedy is that in spite of God's faithfulness to Israel (1 Kgs 8:23), most references to the covenant in 1 and 2 Kings are of Israel's rejection of it. King Solomon, appointed as leader and example of the people of God, fails to keep the covenant (1 Kgs 11:11). Elijah's lament recalls the incessant indictment of the book of Judges that the people had forsaken the covenant (1 Kgs 19:11, 14). Finally, the northern kingdom is judged for rejecting the covenant with God (2 Kgs 17:35, 38; 18:12).

Worship

To give honor to the senior partner in the covenant, to protect his name and reputation as a faithful client, and to ascribe to him his proper attributes are the correct actions and attitudes of the vassal. In religious terms, this is called "worship." The Decalogue, so fundamental to Israel's life and faith, begins with the words

> 'I am the LORD your God, who brought you out of the land of Egypt, out of the house of bondage. You shall have no other gods before me. You shall not make for yourself a graven image, or any likeness of anything that is in heaven above, or that is on the earth beneath, or that is in the water under the earth; you shall not bow down to them or serve them; for I the LORD your God am a jealous God.' (Deut 5:6–9a)

This encapsulates the commitment involved in a covenant relationship. It involves exclusive honor to one, not favors scattered promiscuously to many. God is Israel's God, and Israel is God's people.

Given the nature of a covenant relationship, the terms used of the attitude of one partner to another are personal ones like "serve" ('abad), "fear" (yareh), and "love" ('aheb). These terms are staples of the vocabulary of Deuteronomy and the deuteronomistic history.

Outward forms of worship pertaining to the covenant were the temple in Jerusalem, which stood as a symbol of God's abiding presence with the people; the sacrificial system, by which the worshiper could be absolved of sin or express his devotion to God; and the ark of the covenant, always a reminder of God's commitment and faithfulness to Israel.

Important though these outward forms were, a more important element was a will to worship on the part of the people—the right attitude of heart and mind, and subsequent behavior consistent with what was said and done in worship. It is the judgment of the writer of Kings that this will was mostly absent from Israel. Solomon's heart was turned away from God (1 Kgs 11:2), and this was not simply a temporary lapse of attention, but a deliberate, willful, and consistent attitude (1 Kgs 11:11). Most subsequent kings followed suit.

The reforms carried out by some were unsuccessful not because they were not well-intentioned, but because the general will of the people was otherwise. At least, that was the opinion of their own prophets. When the people were taken into exile, the cause for judgment was simple: They did not worship God. They did not give to God the service, the fear, and the love which was rightfully his. Elijah's complaint in 2 Kings 1 that the king does not know that "there is a God in Israel" is sounded time and again throughout their history.

In the final analysis, since Israel's heart was not willing to worship, the symbols lost their validity, and our writer ends

The People of God

his history of the people with the sad picture of the city, temple, and people being plundered and destroyed by a foreigner. This sets a serious theological problem before us. Knowing what we do of the chosenness of Israel and the covenant-faithfulness (ḥesed) of God, what significance does this have for the future of the people? We shall attempt an answer to this in a later chapter, but first we turn to another important topic, that of the land.

5   THE COVENANTED LAND

The land which Israel occupied for much of her early history, and which she eventually lost, has an importance in world history far beyond its size. Geographically, the land forms part of the fertile crescent, that great arc of watered and arable land which stretches from the northern shore of the modern Arabian Gulf, along the valley of the Tigris and Euphrates Rivers and along the eastern shore of the Mediterranean Sea, until it reaches the border of Egypt at Wadi el-Arish (the Brook of Egypt in the Old Testament). The land occupied by Israel comprises only a small section of this great crescent, and in the frequently noted limits of "Dan to Beersheba," the land was about the size of the state of Vermont.

But that small tract of land formed a vital link in the crescent, which was a major trading route of the ancient world. Historically, it was a link between the great civilizations and empires of North Africa (Egypt) and the land of

Akkad (Assyria and Babylon). It frequently passed into the hands of one or the other, relieved by brief periods of "independence" when the threats and problems were more local.

Beyond this, however, the Bible looks on this land as a symbol, a gift from God and an integral element in the covenant relationship between God and the people. It is at the center of the promise to Abraham (Gen 15:7; 17:1-8). It is the goal of the Exodus (Exod 3:7-12), and with the systematic conquest under Joshua, the land is received as a gift. When Israel had settled in the land, there developed a basic understanding of the relationship between people and land which is so important in the Old Testament. Here, in the land, Israel can find rest and peace (Josh 21:44). The subsequent relationship between the people and the land was perceived in such a way that any threat to the land, any invasion or penetration of its borders, was understood as a serious threat to the covenant community itself. Therefore, during the period of the judges such invasions were resisted with force. During the period of the monarchy this perception was strengthened by the establishment of fortresses and garrisons along the borders (1 Kgs 9:15), the development of a strong physical center (Jerusalem, temple, and palace), and the growth of the status of the king, especially under David and Solomon.

This was a safe land (2 Sam 7:8-11), a prosperous land (Deut 8:7-10) that was given, not earned (Deut 8:17, 18). It is in this light that the "ordnance survey" of the land in Joshua 13-19 is to be understood. The lists of place names and geographical features is confusing and at times tiresome to read, but the main point the reader should bear in mind here is that Joshua's division of the land, at God's command, is part of the covenant agreement. The land is a gift to all the people; therefore, all the people have a proportionate share in the land. In a sense, this passage represents a kind of land reform program in which the land once controlled by the Canaanite city-kings is distributed to the people of Israel as a gesture of God's covenant grace and love. It is against this briefly sketched background that the understanding of the land in 1 and 2 Kings ought to be seen.

Center and boundaries

If, as many interpreters have suggested, the opening chapters of 1 Kings are part of the "succession history" of David and Solomon, then this helps explain why the notion of land is replaced by the term "kingdom" (*mamlakah*) in these early chapters. The use of "kingdom" reflects the new political reality in Israel after David. The gift of the land is now under the control of a central figure, the king (1 Kgs 2:12, 15, 22).

This politically controlled territory is, however, larger than the original gift. Solomon inherited a territory which extended farther north than the boundaries established in Numbers 34:1–12, as being from the Brook of Egypt to Lebo-hamath (not "entrance to Hamath" as in so many modern translations). Solomon's northern border extended to the Euphrates and to the city of Tiphsah (1 Kgs 4:24). Neither of these northern limits corresponds with the northern tribal allotments in Joshua 19, and the differences probably reflect the changing fortunes of Israel throughout her history. Boundaries, while defended and often delineated, were rarely stable. However, the climax of the reign of Solomon, seen in his building of the temple and in his prayer in 1 Kings 8, clearly shows that he did not inherit this extended kingdom by accident, but rather that it is the culmination of the promise to David, and it is bound up with the covenant.

Blessed be the LORD, the God of Israel, who with his hand has fulfilled what he promised with his mouth to David my father. (1 Kgs 8:15)

The Covenanted Land

At the center of this land stands a new and important symbol associated with the reign and activities of Solomon, namely the temple. Its importance for our writer is reflected in the space he devotes to its careful construction (1 Kgs 6:1-38). In the very center of the temple stands the ark representing the covenant between God and the people (1 Kgs 8:1-14). But the temple has a greater significance. In keeping with the numerous promises in the book of Deuteronomy (e.g., Deut 12:5, 6), it is the place God has chosen to dwell with his people, and the focus of his care and concern, his hearing of prayer (1 Kgs 8:27-30). Thus it is that the prayer spoken "toward the city which thou hast chosen and the house which I have built for thy name" upholds the army in battle (1 Kgs 8:44, 45) and brings forgiveness to the repentant sinner (1 Kgs 8:46-53).

The symbolic limits of this land can be extended, either through marriage and political alliance (1 Kgs 3:1-2), or through the inclusion of a non-Israelite, a foreigner (noker) who acknowledges the sovereignty of Israel's God (1 Kgs 8:41-43). This land is important, as is the place of the people in it, and one of the strongest punishments meted out by Solomon is to displace a person, to banish him from Jerusalem (1 Kgs 2:26).

Use and mismanagement

Walter Brueggemann, in his excellent book The Land, makes a distinction between the land as gift and the land as "managed"—by which he means the overtly human element in the treatment of the land.[1] It is the element of controlling the land, as opposed to depending upon it, of selfish use as opposed to grateful use. Part of the understanding of land in 1 and 2 Kings involves this element of "management" of land, and the writer shows a close connection between the misuse of the land and the people's misfortune.

In the account of Solomon's reign there is a paragraph outlining Solomon's organization of the country for purposes of taxation (1 Kgs 4:7-19). The report of the tax divisions is found in a lengthy narrative giving details of Solomon's administration, the amount of provisions needed for his court, and his reputation for wisdom (1 Kgs 4:1-5:14 [4:1-34]). The administrative structure is slightly larger than David's (2 Sam 8:15-18), and includes the office of "minister of forced labor." The administrative divisions for the purposes of taxation number twelve, but do not follow the territorial allotments for the tribes. They are clearly in the interest of efficiency, and to ensure this, some of the local governors are related to the king (Dor and Hazor).

On purely political and economic grounds, given the realities of Solomon's day, one might argue in favor of Solomon's policies. But the perspective of the writer is not purely political, and he is aware that this disregard for the older tribal allotments, coupled with the absence of Judah from the districts obliged to pay taxes, does not bode well for the land. The distribution of the land in keeping with the covenant is now being ignored. The absence from the narrative of any command from God that might legitimize Solomon's actions highlights the contrast between his actions and proper use of the land.

A similar case of "management" comes with the choice of a new northern capital, Samaria (1 Kgs 16:24). The older capital, Tirzah, was replaced by a newly created city, built on the hill of Shemer and fortified. We can only guess at the reasons for the new choice. Perhaps Samaria was closer to the international trade routes. It was certainly more central, and had clear access to the coast. Whatever the reasons, archaeological excavation at the site has shown that the new capital was an impressive city with large, well-made walls. What is clear is that the choice was made by Omri and Omri alone. Although Samaria became the capital city of the north, unlike

Jerusalem in the south it could claim no special status of having been chosen by God. It is never the place "where God dwells." It is one of Omri's "works of greatness" (1 Kgs 16:27), a human construction, made without reference to God.

The third case is probably one of the most famous in 1 Kings, the story of Naboth's vineyard and its expropriation by Ahab and his wife Jezebel (1 Kgs 21). The story is well-known and the details do not need to be repeated. What is most interesting is the challenge made by the prophet Elijah. It is clear from his question (1 Kgs 21:19) that Elijah does not see this action as simply a case of criminal theft, for he alludes to the covenant Law, the Decalogue, and by implication accuses Ahab of breaking that law (cf. Deut 5:17, 21). His choice of words is precise: Ahab is guilty of killing a fellow Israelite without cause (*ratsach*). Management of land, in this case the redistribution of land for selfish gain, is a breach of the covenant, a misuse of the gift, and for this sin Ahab is to be judged.

Shrinking limits

Throughout Israel's history, the boundaries of the land frequently fluctuate, and very often are penetrated by enemies. At times, these shifts in the borders are deliberate and result from the willful action of Israelite kings; but at other times these shifts are the result of circumstances beyond the control of Israel's kings, and are often seen as a precursor of judgment. In both types of cases, however, there is often the sense that the shifts are wrong, ill-advised, and carried out for reasons which have little, if anything, to do with the concept of land as covenanted gift.

Solomon's reign is eventually judged to have been a failure, not because he was politically inept, but because his heart was "turned aside." He lost a sense of perspective, and this loss is set clearly within the context of the numerous alliances through marriages with the daughters of foreign kings (1 Kgs 11:1-7). In this way foreigners are introduced into the land and domain of Israel, but not in the sense of Solomon's own prayer (1 Kgs 8:41-43). These foreigners do not acknowledge Israel's God. On the contrary, they bring with them their own gods and set up their idols, polluting Israel's faith and witness. The same thing is seen in the marriage of Omri to Jezebel of Tyre (1 Kgs 16:29-34). This union results in the attempt by the queen to annihilate the prophetic witness to Israel's God in the northern kingdom.

In 1 Kings 15:9-24, further willful redistribution of the land is carried out as the result of costly and unnecessary wars between Israel and Judah. The outcome is the annexation of Benjamin by Judah, and the introduction of the Syrian king Ben-hadad into the local politics of Israel and Judah when the southern king Asa appeals to him for help. He responds for the price of large tracts of covenanted land in the north. The subsequent wars between Israel and Syria (1 Kgs 20; 22) degenerate into trials of strength between two nations, with little reference to God's will. When God's will is revealed to Jehoshaphat and Ahab through the prophet Micaiah ben Imlah, it is ignored in favor of the kings' wishes, with disastrous results (1 Kgs 22).

In addition to these willful changes in the limits of the land there is a series of changes which are beyond the control of Israel and Judah, the result of invasions by stronger powers. Throughout, there is little appeal to God. Soon after the division of the kingdom into the separate nations of Israel and Judah, the Egyptian Pharaoh Shishak (Sheshonk) invaded (1 Kgs 14:25-28). According to the writer of 1 Kings, Jerusalem was the target and suffered badly at the hands of the invader. But the Egyptian's own account shows the full extent of his raid. He attacked the Negev desert, took many fortified cities of Israel and Judah along some of the main routes, and returned to Egypt unopposed.

59

In spite of David's subjugation of the Philistines (2 Sam 4-5), pressure is reapplied in the south and west by these people (1 Kgs 15:27; 16:15-20), and time and effort must be spent containing them. In the east Syrians lay claim to Is-raelite territory (1 Kgs 20:1-6) and begin a series of wars which are fought back and forth in each country.

Chapters 15-17 of 1 Kings are taken up with a new and more dangerous pressure now exerted by the imperial army of Assyria. After the north falls to the armies of Shalmaneser and Sargon in 722 B.C., Assyrian attention is eventually turned to the south during the reign of Hezekiah (2 Kgs 18-20). The net result is a loss of territory and the destruction of numerous fortified cities. Finally, the Babylonians invade twice and effect the fall of Jerusalem, as well as the looting and destroying of the temple (2 Kgs 24, 25).

Rarely in these narratives is appeal made to God for help—and when it is, as in the case of Hezekiah, the motives are clearly warped. Throughout this history of invasion it is clear that Israel and Judah are vulnerable. The sense of "rest from enemies round about" is destroyed. There is occasional respite, and at times old borders are restored, wounds are healed, and invasions are stemmed. But this happens not because Israel's army was reorganized, or because the two nations fought better. The reason is the same one which gave Israel life and existence in the first place, the grace and mercy of God. It was by the Word of God that Israel de-feated the Syrians (1 Kgs 20:13-34). It was by the grace and mercy of God that Israel, under Jeroboam II, was able to restore the borders once again to Lebo-Hamath (2 Kgs 14:17-27).

Land and loss

We suggested earlier that our writer's task in composing 1 and 2 Kings was to offer an explanation for the Exile. The

Exile meant loss of the land, as well as the other symbols of the covenant, because of invasions by the Assyrians in the latter years of the eighth century B.C. and by the Babylonians in the opening decades of the sixth century B.C. The people of the northern kingdom were scattered throughout the Assyrian empire and were replaced by different groups from other parts of the empire. The result was an admixture of customs and religions which virtually destroyed the old faith. In the south, the Babylonians took away the leading citizens of the population to work within the infrastructure of their own empire. Thus the southern nation lost its effective political and religious leadership.

But this is a descriptive, historical sketch. Other questions remain. What did it mean for the existence of Israel as God's people? What did the destruction of her most cherished symbols of covenant signify? Was it possible for Israel to be Israel away from her covenanted land? These and many other questions must have plagued the exiles. Some of the questions are not answered by the writer of Kings, but are tackled by other writers of the Exile and postexilic period. However, in his interpretation of what happened, our writer lays a strong foundation upon which these later writers could build.

He is writing from the perspective of one in exile, and at a time when the loss was a reality. He understands these events within the context of the covenant and the relationship of the land to the covenant. Put as simply as possible, the loss is a result of the breaking of the covenant relationship, and a forfeiture of its benefits. This is a principle with which he is already familiar because it is set out clearly in his "charter," the book of Deuteronomy (Deut 4:25–31). For making graven images, for forsaking their covenant God, the people will be scattered among the nations. There they will be forced to worship "no-gods" of wood and stone. In a sense, it is what they have already chosen for themselves.

Already in the account of the reign of Solomon the theme is picked up in numerous allusions to the continued faithfulness of the king (or lack of it) and the fate of the land. In 1 Kings 6:11-13 Solomon is reminded that if he walks before God as David walked, in obedience to the Torah, God "will dwell among the children of Israel, and will not forsake my people Israel" (v 13).

The conditional nature of the relationship is clear, and the danger of disobedience is obvious. In his dedicatory prayer, Solomon acknowledges the possibility of exile (1 Kgs 8:46-53). When the people sin, if they repent and pray, Solomon implores God to

> then hear thou in heaven, and forgive the sin of thy people Israel, *and bring them again into the land which thou gavest to their fathers.* (1 Kgs 8:34 italics mine)

Exactly the same theme is repeated in a much extended form in 1 Kings 8:46-51. Here is a precursor of what eventually happened at the end of the monarchy.

Also in the account of the reign of Solomon is a longer exposition of David's deathbed command to his son (1 Kgs 2:1-4). In 1 Kings 9:1-9 the responsibility of Solomon the king is amplified, and the fate of the entire people is brought under his responsibility, for if he, as leader, sins,

> then I will cut off Israel from the land which I have given them; and the house which I have consecrated for my name I will cast out of my sight; and Israel will become a proverb and a byword among all peoples. (1 Kgs 9:7)

Already then in the account of the reign of Solomon, the writer has established the precarious nature of the covenant relationship. Loyalty to the covenant—and to the covenant

God—is crucial for the survival of the relationship, and for the continued enjoyment of the covenant benefits. The question raised in the opening chapters of Kings is whether the relationship can survive the next several hundred years of monarchy.

In the remainder of the narrative of 1 Kings, the theme lies dormant. We have already looked at incidents of lost land (1 Kgs 9:10-14), broken land (1 Kgs 11:9-13), border pressure (1 Kgs 11:14-40), and border penetration (1 Kgs 14:25-28), as well as the reasons for these events. At times, individual kings and their dynasties ("houses") are judged (1 Kgs 14:4-16), but nothing more is said of the loss of the entire land.

With the opening of the narrative of 2 Kings, the theme reemerges. The opening words of 2 Kings 1 again introduce into Israel's history the nation of Moab, which is now in rebellion against Israel. The rebellion is described more fully in chapter 3, and the juxtaposition of this loss with the years following the death of Ahab, Israel's archapostate, is significant. The opportunity for improvement after his reign is lost, and things get worse. In 2 Kings 8:20-22 Judah loses both Edom and the border city of Libnah. By 2 Kings 10:28-36, the reign of Jehu—which had begun with such good intentions—ends with the loss of a substantial part of Israel's territory on the east side of the Jordan River. The Syrian threat continues, and is stayed only because of the compassion of God (2 Kgs 13:22-25).

The greatest historical illustration of the writer's original interpretation of the loss of the land is seen in the eventual destruction of the northern kingdom by Assyria in 722 B.C. This destruction was preceded by several invasions and incursions into Israelite territory. But in 722 Israel fell victim to the inhuman Assyrian policy of splitting up communities of people and scattering them throughout the empire. The policy effectively destroyed any cohesive resistance, and had a devastating effect upon the victims. It resulted in the collapse of all social structure, and it forced the intermingling of nations and customs. It meant the annihilation of a community.

The writer's interpretation of these tragic events is simple. He revives the notion that the loss of land and national identity is the result of the willful rejection of the covenant relationship (2 Kgs 17:7-18). The catalogue of sins found within this chapter echoes again and again the prohibitions of Deuteronomy (WBC 13:219-41). By the same token he anticipates the fate of Judah with his simple statement in verse 19, "But not even Judah kept the commandments of God. They copied exactly what Israel had done."

The subsequent history of Judah follows the reigns of Hezekiah, Manasseh, Amon, Josiah, and the collection of kings who bring the account to an end (Jehoahaz, Jehoiakim, Jehoiachin, and Zedekiah), and there is little in these stories to give hope. Hezekiah allowed the Babylonian emissaries to view the national treasures, symbolically anticipating their plunder later by Nebuchadrezzar (2 Kgs 20:12-19). In spite of his attempted reforms, Manasseh took Judah to depths never before seen (2 Kgs 21:1-17). And despite the valiant attempts of Josiah (2 Kgs 22, 23), Judah's restoration to a covenant relationship was ultimately impossible. It becomes only a matter of time before Judah suffers the same fate as Israel.

To summarize, the writer of Kings seeks to explain how the covenant land was lost. Since possession of the land was dependent on keeping the covenant, breaking the covenant jeopardized tenure of the land. Persistent disobedience and disloyalty brought that tenure to an (albeit temporary) end. To see whether this picture holds any hope for the future for Israel and the land, we must first examine in more detail our writer's notion of sin and judgment.

6 SIN AND JUDGMENT

Examining the topics of sin and judgment more closely and in a more systematic way reveals the reason for the Exile and the loss of the land. In other words, here we touch the question of meaning for the deuteronomist, and this meaning encompasses the life (and potential death) of the people of God, and their role in the passage of events. These themes then are of the greatest importance in understanding the books of 1 and 2 Kings.

The language of sin

Within the language of ancient Israel there was an entire vocabulary relevant to doing right and wrong, and to the sanctions that were applied to wrongdoers as well as the benefits which came to the righteous. This language was not limited to what we would term "ethics"; what it encompassed was far broader. It involved the practice of justice, individual and social ethics, and religion—not as separate institutions, but rather as areas of life which were closely intermingled. An infraction of the rules of behavior regarding any area of life was regarded as a "sin," against which sanctions were applied. 1 and 2 Kings uses four words for such infractions.

In order of frequency, the first is 'asham, which is used only once (2 Kgs 12:17), without explanation. The term is usually translated "guilt," but we must be careful not to read into this term the Western psychological understanding of guilt as a feeling of having done wrong. "Guilt" in this context is more an attribute. According to Leviticus 5:15–19 it can be removed by an offering of a certain value, a tax paid to the priests and restitution to the one offended. During the reforms of Jehoash, some adjustment is made in the system of payment of the "guilt money" (2 Kgs 12:17). The context for the guilt payment seems to be that of a wrong done to others, and has little to do with our writer's exposition of Israel's sin and judgment.

The Hebrew word 'awon occurs in 1 Kings 8:47; 17:18; and 2 Kings 7:9. It is often translated as "sin" or "wrongdoing." The first occurrence in Kings is in the dedicatory prayer of Solomon, wherein Israel is to repent of her sin as the first step to restoration. The second occurrence is in the woman of Zarephath's verbal attack on Elijah after the death of her son. This death, she believes, is a result of her "sin" which Elijah has now brought back to notice by his presence in her house. The third of these occurrences is in the words of the lepers who are looting the deserted Syrian encampment. By not sharing their good fortune with other Israelites they are doing wrong and their 'awon will overtake them (see also Num 32:23). In other words, they will be punished for it. In the case of both 'asham and 'awon (which are common elsewhere in the Old Testament), the writer of 1 and 2 Kings shares assumptions about their meanings with other Old Testament writers, and neither is explained.

The two remaining words are used in association with other words and are placed in certain contexts to give them broader application. In 1 Kings 8:50 the word *pesha'* is translated "transgression." The word is found in six other places, but in quite different, and nonreligious, contexts. In 1 Kings 12:19 it is used to describe the secession of the northern tribes from the united monarchy. It is an act of "rebellion." In 2 Kings 1:1; 3:5, 7 it is used similarly of the declaration of independence of Moab. For several years, probably since the time of David, Moab had been a vassal territory to Israel, and shortly after the death of Ahab, Moab successfully rebelled against Israel. Israelite-built cities were destroyed, Israelite inhabitants were slaughtered or enslaved, and Israelite rule was thrown off. Precisely the same word is used to describe the same action taken by Edom not long after this (2 Kgs 8:20, 22).

In applying this term to the action of Israel against God, the writer has used a metaphor from the realm of international politics—the same realm from which "covenant" was taken. Israel's sin against God was that of willful rebellion, an expression of the desire to be free of the relationship that bound the people and God together. This is, of course, a clearly prophetic view of the relationship between God and the people. This is the action of a people who honor with their lips, but whose heart (i.e., will) is far from obedient (Isa 29:13), a people who "long ago . . . broke your yoke and burst your bonds; and . . . said, 'I will not serve'" (Jer 2:20).

The fourth word which is used of the sinful action of the people is the most common, occurring almost eighty times in 1 and 2 Kings. It is the Hebrew word *chat'ah*, normally translated "sin." In 1 and 2 Kings the word first appears in the prayer of Solomon at the dedication of the temple (1 Kgs 8:22–53). This section of 1 Kings has long been recognized as a programmatic statement, outlining the theological perspective of the deuteronomist, so it is an important place to start. The exposition of the term here shows it to refer to an act against God (1 Kgs 8:46) or to an action committed against

Sin and Judgment

another Israelite, a "neighbor" (1 Kgs 8:31). The word represents an action for which there are serious consequences. Defeat in battle and loss of honor can result (1 Kgs 8:33). Natural disasters, such as drought, can even be blamed on *chat'ah* (1 Kgs 8:35). But there is more to be said. The willful nature of the action is seen in the prayer of repentance in 1 Kings 8:47, "We have sinned, and have acted perversely and wickedly." The same point is clearly made again in 1 Kings 8:50.

From this point on in 1 and 2 Kings, the vast majority of occurrences of the term concern one specific manifestation of *chat'ah*, and that is what we have come to understand as *apostasy*. In its English form, the word derives from the Greek meaning "to stand outside, or apart from" something. In the Old Testament, it is the opposite of repentance (*shubh*). It is a "turning away" (*meshubah*) from God, which seems to have been a word coined by Jeremiah (Jer 3:6, 8, 11, 12; 8:5). With the use of this compound of the verb "to turn" (*shubh*) the element of deliberate and willful action is retained. This particular manifestation of *chat'ah* casts an unavoidable shadow over the unfolding history of Israel and Judah.

It is the "great sin" (2 Kgs 17:21) of the first king of the northern nation, Jeroboam, who set up idols in the north as rivals for God (1 Kgs 12:25–33). It is also this sin which stains the whole of the subsequent life of the northern nation. King after king is given the dubious distinction of following in Jeroboam's footsteps and encouraging Israel to reject Yahweh, the God of the Exodus (e.g., 1 Kgs 14:16; 15:26, 30, 34; 16:26; 2 Kgs 10:29, 31; 13:2, 11; 14:24; 15:9, 18, 24, 28). In the south, Manasseh is credited with the same pervasive influence.

> Moreover Manasseh shed very much innocent blood . . . besides the sin which he made Judah to sin so that they did what was evil in the sight of the LORD. (2 Kgs 21:16)

In the narrative of the struggle for succession to David's throne, one further shaft of light is shed on the term's meaning. When Adonijah had begun preparations for his coronation as David's successor, Bathsheba approached the dying king with a plea for herself and her son. She reminded the king that he had promised the throne to Solomon, and asked him to make good his promise, "Otherwise it will come to pass, when my lord the king sleeps with his fathers, that I and my son Solomon will be counted offenders" (1 Kgs 1:21). The word translated "offenders" is a form of the word *chat'ah*, namely *chat'aim*, a word elsewhere translated "sinners" (Ps 51:15 [51:13]). Bathsheba was clearly concerned about her status in the royal court. If Adonijah became king, she and her family would be regarded as outsiders, illegitimate claimants to the throne and not a part of the inner group, the holders of power. She feared the attribution to her and her family of willful rejection of the king's authority. This use, incidentally, is remarkably close to the religious authorities' use of the term "sinner" in the Gospels.

Regardless of the different terms for "sin" in 1 and 2 Kings, two points emerge. The first is that the act of sin is a deliberate, willful action. It involves a choice—and in the case of Israel and Judah, the choice made was the wrong one. The second is that throughout this story we are never far away from sin as the cause for the destruction of a relationship, in most cases the destruction of the relationship between God and the people. In other words, we are never far away from the principles of the covenant. Before exploring this further, we ought to turn to an examination of the role of Torah in the theme of sin and judgment.

Sin, judgment, and law

There is little doubt that the concept of Torah (translated "Law" in most English versions) is of great importance to the

69

writer of 1 and 2 Kings. We have suggested that the standard by which he judges Israel and Judah is the book of Deuteronomy, a book of Torah. At the very beginning of the story of the reign of Solomon he sets out his presuppositions clearly when he records David's charge to Solomon:

> Keep the charge of the LORD your God, walking in his ways and keeping his statutes, his commandments, his ordinances, and his testimonies, as it is written in the law [Torah] of Moses, that you may prosper in all that you do and wherever you turn. (1 Kgs 2:3)

In some forms of Christian theology the concept of Law has received a rather negative image, reduced by some simply to a tool to point out sin. This is a rather unfair image, and it is in complete contrast to the sense of joy which surrounds the meditation on Torah in Psalm 119: "Open my eyes, that I may behold wondrous things out of thy law [Torah]" (v 18); and again: "In the way of thy testimonies I delight as much as in all riches . . . I will delight in thy statutes; I will not forget thy word" (vv 14–16). Even today Jews celebrate the role of the Torah in their life with the annual festival of Simhat Torah, "rejoicing in the Torah."

Part of our problem is that we narrow the concept too much to fit our modern, Western idea of what "Law" is, or should be, and we fail to appreciate the breadth of the term in the Old Testament. For us, laws are made by legislative bodies, usually elected by the people. We make a rigid distinction between civil and criminal law, and between private morality and legislated public behavior. Courts are distinct institutions, and their officers are distinct persons. Their behavior and functioning are accompanied by types of ceremonies. Courts have "police" powers to enforce their decisions. For us, law is absolute and impartial (symbolized by blind justice), and a court case is usually adversarial, with one participant winning and the other losing.

We take this form of law and justice for granted, but in the world of the Old Testament, few, if any, of these presuppositions would be held. Some laws were legislated by the king, but there are few examples of this in the Old Testament. Distinctions between private and public morality, between civil and criminal law, and between sacred and secular law were nonexistent. The roles of the Old Testament judges were ambiguous, and the office seems to have been a slowly evolving one. While justice was often done "in the gate" (Ruth 4:11; 2 Sam 19:8), this area was not a law court in the modern sense of a separate location dedicated solely to this purpose. The gate was also the meeting place of the elders, and probably the market area of the city. Finally, while the concept of justice may have been an absolute one, the practice of law was dependent much more on negotiation between antagonists in a case, and on the social status, wisdom, and common sense of the arbitrator.

These points are worth pondering because they show the different orientation of the Old Testament system of justice. This orientation was much more toward the maintenance and restoration of relationships. Thus it is that some of the severest penalties were reserved for actions that would destroy social patterns. Actions causing disruption of the family were harshly treated. Actions breaking the barriers that bound the group together were harshly treated. Adultery, which today is reduced to the level of a pastime, was likewise treated severely.

Laws did not apply to all people, only to members of the community. In sum, the Law was not for the protection of the rights of members of society, but rather for the preservation of the community of Israel. If we can understand the different orientation of the Old Testament concept and

Sin and Judgment

system of justice, then we can understand better the use of the term *Torah* in 1 and 2 Kings, and indeed in the entire Old Testament.

Solomon, now head of the people, is charged in 1 Kings 2:3 with a serious responsibility. This charge is repeated in a slightly longer form in 1 Kings 9:4-9. He is to maintain his allegiance to the Torah, and to live according to the Torah in all its breadth and depth. Only then will the throne be retained, and only then will the people prosper and thrive. This is the standard by which Israel and Judah, and their respective kings, will be judged. What is at stake here is not the preservation of law and order, but rather the very existence of the people of God as a chosen and favored people. It is the covenant and Torah which bind the two together.

But the charge to Solomon is not kept, even by Solomon. This is the simple analysis of the deuteronomist. Jehu, who assumed the throne in order to stem the tide of disobedience and apostasy in the north, is himself judged to be a failure. "[He] . . . was not careful to walk in the [Torah] of the Lord the God of Israel with all his heart" (2 Kgs 10:31), and as a result the territory of the community began to crumble away (v 32). The cause of the Exile and destruction of the northern nation is likewise simply stated.

> The LORD warned Israel and Judah by every prophet and every seer, saying, "Turn from your evil ways and keep my commandments. . . . But they would not listen. . . ." (2 Kgs 17:13-14; see also vv 37-40)

Like Israel, Judah too rejected the Torah (2 Kgs 17:19), and produced a king, Manasseh, who rivaled Ahab for his disobedience and apostasy. Of his reign and his people it is stated:

> "I will not cause the feet of Israel to wander any more out of the land which I gave to their fathers, if only

they will be careful to do all that I have commanded them, and according to all the [Torah] that my servant Moses commanded them." But they did not listen, and Manasseh seduced them to do more evil than the nations had done whom the LORD destroyed before the people of Israel. (2 Kgs 21:8–9)

Here we find an important clue to the Exile. Before the reign of Manasseh was over the people had chosen not only to disobey, but to act worse than the Canaanites who preceded them in the land. By rejecting the Torah they had in effect chosen to live as though they had not been favored and chosen by God—as though they had not entered into a covenant with God.

Only two "bad" kings are recorded as having obeyed the Torah in specific incidents. Amaziah of Judah, son of the assassinated Joash, avenged his father's death, but stopped short of extending his vengeance to the children of the assassins. The reason for this was the modification (in Deut 24:16) of the law which dealt with criminal behavior and families (Exod 20:5). The rest of the record of Amaziah's reign is a sad one.

The other obedient king was, of course, Josiah, who embarked on a widespread reform of worship in Judah and in parts of the north, inspired specifically by the instructions of the book of Torah found during the repairs of the temple (2 Kgs 22:8, 11; 23:1, 24).

But it seems that, however well-intentioned these actions were, they were not fully successful. Perhaps a small measure of stability was restored to the community, but in the final analysis two kings could do little to prevent the complete breakdown of community life and worship, or to stem the tide of the Babylonian invasion. Judah suffered the same fate as Israel—invasion and exile from the land—because Judah, like Israel, had rejected the very thing which would have bound the community together and preserved its special identity, the covenant Torah.

Judgment

Seeing the concept of Torah within the context of the covenant helps us in our understanding of the themes of sin and judgment in Kings. Whatever form it takes, judgment is the result of disobedience to the Torah and rejection of the covenant—in other words, a deliberate abandonment of the relationship between the people and God. This act of rebellion is not merely the breaking of law, but a refusal to live within the relationship established by covenant.

This is no light thing, because this relationship alone gave Israel her reason for being, and her distinct character. Israel has no identity apart from God. According to biblical testimony, God is the author of Israel's life. John Goldingay expresses it well:

The notion of election is a key to understanding the notion of Israel. It is not even that God makes an already existent people his own, he brings a people into being. They only exist as a people because of an act of God. . . . What is distinctive about Israel is not that they see themselves as God's people . . . but that they see themselves as Yahweh's people. . . .[1]

The sad commentary made by 1 and 2 Kings is that the very source of Israel's life was rejected. It would be a mistake then to see the concepts of sin and judgment in 1 and 2 Kings as working in a sort of mechanical way, as though there were an automatic penalty for the breaking of a certain rule. The whole matter is much more personal.

If there is a metaphor which epitomizes the covenant relationship in the Old Testament, it is that of family. Sometimes it is seen as being like the relationship between a father and son (Hos 11:1), and as being like the relationship between a husband and wife (Jer 2:1-4). The writer of 1 and 2 Kings does not use these images, but through his knowledge and understanding of the works of the prophets (2 Kgs 17:13) he would have been well aware of them. As we have seen, the notion of covenant is important to the writer's way of interpreting life, and the covenant is at its heart a relationship. Under the tutelage of Manasseh, the people of God chose to live as though they were not the people of God. They abandoned this special relationship. The breaking of such a relationship causes loss of honor and deep pain for the senior partner. On the part of the rebel, there is a forfeiture of the benefits of the relationship. Just as a wayward spouse abandoning the responsibilities of a family also abandons the pleasures, comfort, support, companionship, and shared property of the family, so Israel, in abandoning her covenant relationship, also gave up her right to be called God's special people, as well as the privileges of this unique relationship.

7   HOPE, AND THE ANGER
OF GOD

Context

We have placed the writer of 1 and 2 Kings in the period of
the Exile. His work concludes with Jerusalem being destroyed by the Babylonian army of Nebuchadrezzar, and the
main citizens of the country being taken into Babylon against
their will. A puppet regime was established in Mizpah, but
it soon fell victim to a local nationalist remnant which had
support from the Ammonites. These events took place in 586
B.C. and shortly afterward. The narrative of 1 and 2 Kings
probably was completed within a few years of these events.
The writer was still able to refer to royal and court records in
some form. Other archival material relating to the temple was
cited in detail, and probably not from memory.

Like most good historians, the deuteronomist speaks as
much *to* his own age as *of* the past. His work is an interpretation of the past, and he has shown how the consistent
apostasy of Israel and Judah led to the loss of land, community, and—almost—loss of identity. He reads the past from a

perspective shared by the prophets. He also is one of the first writers of the exilic and postexilic period to seek meaning in the events of the Exile, and to offer a basis for reconstruction. Ralph Klein puts it clearly:

> The task of the hour was for Israel . . . to acknowledge God's justice, to listen to his voice and to do his law. And then, though Dtr even is short on details, Israel could hope that Yahweh, in his unpredictable freedom would act as Savior once more.[1]

The question is, after the writer of Kings' pessimistic view of the history of the people of Israel and Judah from conquest to Exile, does he offer hope for the future? If so, how?

In answering these questions here, we are not dealing with the entire Old Testament message of hope. Much has been written on the way the Old Testament as a whole is forward-looking; that message can be taken for granted. We are dealing rather with the contribution made by this writer to an understanding of God as a God of hope and grace.

The anger of God

At first there seems to be little to relieve initial pessimism because, not only is the judgment of the Exile seen to be the result of a consistent pattern of apostasy, but it is also considered to be the result of an angry reaction on God's part. One Hebrew expression for this reaction is a combination of two words: *charah*, often translated "inflame," and *'aph*, which is the word for "nostril." The term occurs numerous times in other parts of the Old Testament, and three times in 1 and 2 Kings. According to 2 Kings 13:3, this reaction of God's to the sins of Israel was the cause of Israel's defeat at the hands of Hazael of Damascus. This is exactly the same reason given for the numerous invasions and periods of oppression in the book of Judges (Judg 3:7). God has a similar reaction to the activities of Manasseh (2 Kgs 23:26). And it is for this reason that he finally casts Judah out his presence (2 Kgs 24:20).

Another Hebrew expression which captures the same reaction on God's part is a form of the verb ka'as, which is often translated "to provoke to anger." For example, Jeroboam ben Nebat provoked God to anger with his apostasies (1 Kgs 14:9, 15; 15:30). The same is said of Baasha (1 Kgs 16:2, 7, 13), Omri (1 Kgs 16:26), Ahab (1 Kgs 16:33; 21:22), Ahaziah (1 Kgs 22:54 [22:53]), people of Israel (2 Kgs 17:11, 17; 23:19), Manasseh (2 Kgs 21:6, 15; 23:26), and people of Judah (2 Kgs 22:17).

To state as boldly as this that the judgment on the people was a direct result of the anger of God makes it seem as though the action of God was arbitrary, hasty, and vindictive. In fact, this view of God has caused considerable debate and heart-searching among students of the Old Testament for centuries. Some explanations have excused this kind of vocabulary as part of a primitive view of God which was later outgrown. Others have seen it as simply a way of speaking conditioned by the world view of the time, and not to be taken seriously by moderns. Still others have found the whole concept of an angry God offensive, and have rejected it.

Before we pass too hasty a judgment upon the concept, let us consider it further. Several things need to be noted about the Old Testament understanding of the anger of God. The first is that, although some of the same language is used of the anger of God as well as the anger of humans, as Bruce Dahlberg has stated, ". . . there is a qualitative and theological difference between human anger on the one hand and divine anger on the other."[2] Human anger is often viewed negatively in Scripture. It is accepted when it is directed against injustice or exploitation (2 Sam 12:5) or when faith is lacking (2 Kgs 13:19), but in the majority of cases it is seen

79

as an unprofitable attitude. In Genesis 4:5-8 it leads to murder, and in the wisdom literature of the Old Testament (Job, Proverbs, and Ecclesiastes) it is condemned as cruel (Prov 27:4) or as fitting for a fool (Prov 14:17). In contrast to the hot-tempered person, the ideal is the "cool" person (Prov 17:27) who is able to control (but not deny) the emotions. Another aspect of human anger is its irrationality, as seen in the poem condemning the "raging" of the Babylonians against God and God's people (2 Kgs 19:27). This raging is born of arrogance. Another insight into human anger is seen in the childish sulking of the disappointed Ahab when he was chastised by the prophet (1 Kgs 20:43) and when his request was refused by Naboth (1 Kgs 21:4).

The second thing to be noted about the Old Testament understanding of the anger of God is that it is not an attribute in the theological sense, so much as an emotion. Like most emotions described in the Old Testament, anger is revealed by what God does. But this emotion is not an arbitrary one which flares up at the slightest pretext (this is more characteristic of what the Old Testament understands of human anger). It is rather an emotion that is aroused only after the severest provocation. God is "gracious and merciful, slow to anger, and abounding in steadfast love" (Joel 2:13).

The notion of the anger of God is a difficult one to comprehend, especially in a society in which open emotion is traditionally not shown. By way of almost complete contrast, the cultural milieu of the Old Testament is refreshing in the expression of emotion and in the way it describes the expression of emotion. Most of the attitudes and emotions which we would normally describe by referring to some internal, hidden characteristic of the person, the Old Testament describes by referring to some physical, and therefore very public, gesture.

The English "to respect," which does not necessarily have any outward manifestation in our culture, is matched by the expression "to lift the face" in the Old Testament (2 Kgs 5:1). What we would call being "sad" or "depressed," in Hebrew is called having a "fallen face" (Gen 4:6). "To pay attention" is "to give ear to," or "to incline the ear to" (Ps 78:1). For God to be angry is for him to give outward expression to the sense of rejection, to the loss and pain of the broken relationship between him and his people. It is therefore not "incalculable or arbitrary," as was claimed by Rudolf Otto, nor is it divorced from moral issues. As Heschel put it when describing the drive behind the prophetic message, "His anger is aroused when the cry of the oppressed comes to his ears."[3]

Finally, one ought always to bear in mind the moral alternative to an "angry God" in this sense. That is a God without emotion, devoid of feeling and interest in the affairs of human beings—a God who is apathetic. Such a God would not be deserving of worship or of praise.

Hope

The sense of hope in 1 and 2 Kings is expressed in a much more subtle way than is the idea of judgment. The events of the previous few years had given an awful and terrifying reality to the prophets' warnings of judgment. The ruins of the capital city and the devastation of the surrounding countryside were proof enough of the seriousness with which the announcements of judgment were to be taken. But what of the future? Out of these ashes could a new nation, a new people of God, arise? Or, in the words of the psalmist, "Has God forgotten to be gracious? Has he in anger shut up his compassion?" (Ps 77:9).

The writer of Kings did look forward to a continuing future relationship between God and the people (see WBC 13:xxx–xxxviii, 359–69). The writer does not say this in so many words—it is expressed in a much more subtle manner. Through his interpretation of events, the writer sets down a solid foundation upon which later exilic writers can build. Often, in a work of literature the final images are the most dramatic and those impressions are the most lasting; and 1 and 2 Kings is no exception. It would be helpful for us to look again at the closing chapter of 2 Kings.

The question of the relationship of 2 Kings 24-25 to Jeremiah 52 complicates matters (for further study, see WBC 13:359ff). Regardless of source and comparative length, each account of the fall of Jerusalem offers a distinctive contribution to the development of Old Testament themes.

Second Kings 25 is a series of six vignettes about the end of the state of Judah and its institutions. First, the king's fate is recorded (vv 4-7). Next, the city is systematically burned (vv 8-12). Then the temple is burned and looted (vv 13-17). After that, the religious and political leaders are executed (vv 18-21). Then the newly appointed governor is assassinated (vv 22-26). Finally, the "legitimate" king (who had been exiled prior to all of this) is released from prison and treated well in Babylon (vv 27-30).

The message of this series of vignettes is clear—every symbol of religious, civil, or military life in Judah was destroyed. Even the puppet regime of Gedaliah failed, and those who assassinated him did not remain to reconstruct a new society, but fled to Egypt. But all is not lost because some symbols remain intact. The temple vessels and the king, Jehoiachin, although in Babylon, are intact.

The significance of this becomes clear when we recall the building of the temple in 1 Kings 6-8. In all the detail of its construction one important theme resounds: the temple and all its furnishings and utensils combine to symbolize the presence of God with his people (1 Kgs 8:12-15). In its final form, then, this concluding chapter of 1 and 2 Kings presents on the one hand, a picture of the widespread destruction of Judah and Jerusalem, but on the other hand, the continuity of certain symbols of faith in exile in

Babylon. It is clear from contemporary events, such as those described in Jeremiah 27–29, that the presence of these symbols in Babylon was the source of continued hope for the people.

It means, further, that the center of the renewed life of the people was no longer Judah and Jerusalem, but Babylon. As Israel had been called out of Egypt to enter the Land of Promise, so Israel would be called out of the north country and the lands where she had been scattered to enter again the new land of promise (Jer 16:13). In the words of Robert Carroll,

> The deuteronomist's view is, "Only in exile and among the exiles is there hope for the future," but that principle needs to be made more precise so as to reflect the proper nuance of the [writer]. "Only in the Babylonian exile and among the Babylonian exiles is that hope to be found."[4]

Restoring fortunes

Within that literature of the Old Testament which scholars call the deuteronomistic literature, there is a common theme. From the book of Deuteronomy, through the narrative of 1 and 2 Kings, to the book of Jeremiah (whose sections of prose bear a close similarity to the speeches of the deuteronomistic literature), there is anticipation of the continued apostasy of the people, the judgment of the people, and the future restoration of the people. The exposition of this theme in 1 and 2 Kings is but one stage in its development. Let us look at some aspects of this development more closely. We shall briefly examine three passages: Deuteronomy 4:15–31; 1 Kings 8:14–53; and Jeremiah 32:1–44.

In the Introduction, I quoted from the work of Robert Polzin:

Hope, and the Anger of God

It is as though the deuteronomist is telling us in Deuteronomy, "Here is what God has prophesied concerning Israel," but in Joshua–2 Kings, "This is how God's word has been exactly fulfilled in Israel's history from the settlement to the destruction of Jerusalem and the Exile."

With Polzin and others, I view Deuteronomy as an integral part of this masterwork, the so-called deuteronomistic history.

In Deuteronomy 4, toward the end of the first major speech of Moses in the book, the themes of judgment and restoration are addressed head-on. In verses 15–19 Moses warns the people, who are about to enter the land, of the dangers of apostasy and idol-making. The reason is that Israel is Yahweh's special possession (v 20). In verses 21, 22 there is a brief reference to Moses' own fate. Moses was judged for his disobedience, and God, in his anger, refused him entry into the Promised Land. This is an important statement. Even Moses, the architect of the covenant society, is not exempt from the standards God sets out, nor from the penalty for disobedience.

Verses 23, 24 make a statement about the uniqueness of God, and his "jealous" nature. This is followed in verses 25, 26 with another warning against apostasy, and by a prediction of the judgment of exile where the people will "serve gods of wood and stone" (vv 27, 28). In other words, they will have what they wished for! From this position of exile and banishment the people will repent (vv 29, 30), and will be restored because of God's mercy and grace, and because God will not forget the covenant (v 31).

Polzin points out that there is an implied tension between the judgment of God on the one hand, and the mercy of God on the other. In his opinion, this tension is also seen in the way the speech of Moses is constructed. He uses the helpful notion of a "dialogue," two voices struggling with an issue of supreme importance to the readers. On the one hand is "the voice of retributive justice," and on the other, "the voice of unconditional and inexplicable election."[5]

This is a very helpful image to bear in mind because it is repeated again and again throughout the history which follows, and is clearly in evidence in the early chapters of Judges. Here, sin and judgment are juxtaposed with grace and deliverance. In another "speech," this time in the form of a prayer, these two contrasting themes are picked up.

At the scene of the dedication of the temple in 1 Kings 8, the king, Solomon, offers a prayer (vv 14–53) which contains within it much of the language of Moses' speeches in Deuteronomy, as well as many of the same themes. At the same time, the prayer reflects the different setting. Solomon begins his prayer with a summary of God's faithfulness. At the heart of this summary is the promise made to David, concluding with the appeal to David for constant faithfulness. Verses 27–30 contain a brief prayer concerning the temple. This is followed by a series of prayers covering different topics: an offense against a neighbor (vv 31, 32), defeat in battle (vv 33, 34), drought (vv 35, 36), famine (vv 37–40), the arrival of a foreigner (vv 41–43), battle (vv 44, 45), and finally exile because of sin against God (vv 46–53).

In each case raised in the prayer, the potential problem is resolved when prayer toward the place where God dwells is answered. In the case of exile, repentance brings forgiveness and a return to the land. The key is the graciousness and mercy of the God who brought Israel out of Egypt. The dialogue continues, but there is no conflict between the "voices" here, rather, as in a true dialogue, there is a search for meaning and for understanding of the relationship between God's judgment (which seems perfectly justified) and God's mercy (to which Israel's past history gives adequate testimony).

Hope, and the Anger of God

This dialogue is repeated in Jeremiah 32, but with a significant difference. In this narrative, which has all the flavor of deuteronomistic writing, the voices are distinct and a true dialogue merges between the prophet and God himself.

This story of Jeremiah 32 is probably one of the best known in the book of Jeremiah. It is about the purchase of a field in Anathoth at the time of the Babylonian invasion. The story is full of drama. In verses 1-5 the historical setting is given. The city is under siege. Jeremiah had warned of this and for this boldness he was put in prison. The message is ominous and clear, "Behold, I am giving this city into the hand of the king of Babylon" (v 3). The command for Jeremiah to buy his cousin's field in Anathoth (vv 6-8) follows immediately. When the cousin then shows up offering to sell the field, it confirms that the command came from God (v 8).

Jeremiah obeys the command, then receives a hint as to the reason for the order. Given the circumstances, it is surprising.

> For thus says the LORD of hosts, the God of Israel: Houses and fields and vineyards shall again be bought in this land. (Jer 32:15)

This brief explanation stirs Jeremiah to prayer, seeking an answer to this puzzle. In the prayer (vv 16-25), the prophet reviews the past history of God with the people. The pattern is familiar. Although God had rescued Israel from Egypt and given them a land, Israel has disobeyed by rejecting the Torah and now she is suffering the consequences. For much of his previous life Jeremiah had devoted himself to the proclamation of these consequences, so the judgment had come as no surprise to him. What had surprised him was the order to buy land! Notice the sense of confusion in verses 24, 25:

> What thou didst speak has come to pass,
> and behold, thou seest it. Yet thou, O
> LORD GOD, hast said to me, "Buy the field
> for money and get witnesses"—*though
> the city is given into the hands of the Chaldeans.*

The explanation comes in the concluding speech of God in verses 26–44 and consists of three elements. First, Jeremiah is right—the judgment of God upon the people was justified, and in this section of the response there is an extended exposition of the nature of the apostasy of Judah, similar to the accusations brought against Israel in 2 Kings 17. Second, God will bring the people back to the land and will renew his covenant with them (vv 36–41). Third, and most important, this is not the action of a confused God, but of the same God who brought Israel into existence in the first place.

He is just, but also merciful.

> For thus says the LORD: Just as I have brought all this great evil upon this people, so I will bring upon them all the good that I promise them. . . . for I will restore their fortunes, says the LORD. (Jer 32:42–44)

God's anger reveals his reaction to sin, but his fundamental disposition is still one of grace.

The understanding of the Exile in 1 and 2 Kings cannot be seen apart from this broader understanding of judgment and exile in the entire work of the deuteronomist. The historical events he is interpreting needed to be seen for what they were—the judgment of God upon an apostate people. But it is the judgment of a God who had graciously brought this nation into existence, saved her from slavery, bound himself to her in covenant, and given her a land. Such a God does not give up easily.

The writer sets the stage already for the return from exile in Deuteronomy 4 and in 1 Kings 8, reminding the reader occasionally throughout his narrative of the gracious, saving action of God. He saved them from enemies in the time of the judges (Judg 2:18). He promised to answer their prayers of repentance (1 Kgs 8:46-53). He rescued them on a number of occasions from the attacks of hostile neighbors (2 Kgs 13:4-6; 22, 23). He extended their borders even under the reign of an apostate king (2 Kgs 14:23-26) and turned back the might of the Assyrian army when Judah was threatened with extinction (2 Kgs 18:13-19:37). Even in exile there was a sense of continuity with the existence of the temple utensils.

These symbols of the presence of God were indeed important, but the hope for the future was seen even more in the continuity of God's involvement in the life of the people. The action of judgment was the action of a God who had time and again shown that he cared for his people. His behavior was consistent with what had been revealed before. The judgment was no arbitrary act, nor was it an abandonment of his heritage. Had it been either of these, there would be no grounds for hope. As it was, with his exposition of the temporary nature of the Exile, hope was kept alive.

8 CONCLUSION

The writer of 1 and 2 Kings composed a skillfully penetrat-
ing narrative through which his readers could view, and understand, their past. As part of the deuteronomistic history, 1
and 2 Kings follows the pattern of narrative interspersed with
summary speeches, prayers, or lengthy editorial comment.
Robert Polzin's book *Moses and the Deuteronomist* examines
the mode of writing and composition from the books of
Deuteronomy through Joshua, and later studies have traced
this pattern through other parts of the history. In the commentary (WBC 13:xvi–xix), I examined this and other features of the writer's style and technique, as did Professor
DeVries (WBC 12:xxxviii–xlix). Recently, a fine essay on 1
and 2 Kings, written by George Savran, was published in the
important volume, *The Literary Guide to the Bible*. This essay
is highly recommended.[1]

It is important to appreciate that the books of 1 and 2
Kings are not simply a repository of stories about favorite
individual Judeans or Israelites. While Solomon is an important (and somewhat tragic) figure, we do the narrative a

disservice by extracting the stories about him and treating them, whether in sermon or Bible study, as though they were without context. The same is true of Elijah or Elisha. These prophetic giants must be seen within the grand sweep of Israel's history from conquest to Exile. They are part of the sad decline of the people of God, and their strong voices of opposition raised against injustice and apostasy serve to heighten the tragic seriousness of that decline. As the writer himself points out, the people had been warned continually by the prophets, yet still persisted in their willful waywardness (2 Kgs 17:13, 14). This is in fact the heart of the writer's message. In our survey of themes we have kept this in mind and sought to see what the entire narrative of 1 and 2 Kings contributes to our understanding of the role of kings, prophets, people, land, sin, judgment, and hope.

Our writer also takes the past very seriously, and in this regard he can rightly be called a historian. It would be impossible in this volume to become involved in the wide-ranging and complicated debate on the meaning and practice of history. The debate will continue for many years to come. Again, in the commentary on 2 Kings I examined some of the features of this debate (WBC 13:xxx-xxxviii), and DeVries examined the issues in his volume (WBC 12:xxix-xxxviii). The writer did not pen the history of ancient Israel in the same way a modern historian would, but he could hardly be expected to do that. George Savran understands history correctly as "a selection of details, the imposition of a pattern of organization, and the expression of a historian's point of view."[2] Modern historians would select different details, impose a different pattern of organization, and express a different point of view, but that does not make the older way of writing any less valuable as history. At a time when much of what passes for history is the collecting of masses of data—much of it without connection or meaning—it is refreshing to read something which paints a picture in large but recognizable strokes. As the boy in Dylan Thomas's Christmas essay found out, it is disappointing to receive each year "books that told me everything about the wasp, except why."

The writer of 1 and 2 Kings writes to understand and to inform, but he also writes with a deep passion. His passion is born of the fact that he writes about his own people and his own God and the relationship between the two. As Abraham Heschel said,

> To comprehend what phenomena are, it is important to suspend judgment and think in detachment; to comprehend what phenomena mean, it is necessary to suspend indifference and be involved.[3]

If the writer may be called "prophetic" in any sense of the word, then he wrote with what Heschel called "prophetic pathos," and this moves him out of the role of "pure historian."

> The prophets do not offer reflections about ideas in general. Their words are onslaughts, scuttling illusions of false security, challenging evasions, calling faith to account, questioning prudence and impartiality.[4]

Prophets, whether they proclaim their words from the rooftops, in the marketplaces, or, as our writer does, through story, are an embarrassment. They make us uncomfortable because they deal with the issues of life that really matter. The "bottom line" for our writer is the state of the relationship of his people to God, and nothing is more basic. He writes as a believer, as part of that people.

The writer's belief is not born simply from a reflection on his people's past, from which he can draw conclusions. His belief is born rather of a contemplation of the biblical

God—the God of Abraham, Isaac, and Jacob; the God of Moses, Gideon, and Samuel. This God is not narrowly defined, nor is his truth limited, as the hymn writer stated, "to our poor reach of mind." This is a God beyond human understanding (and control)—a God who reveals himself in action and word, and who makes no excuses for himself.

There is here—as in all contemplation of the nature, character, and activity of God—an element of deep mystery. That God should judge his people is a mystery, but so is the fact that he should love them in the first place. That he then chooses to restore and bless broadens the mystery. In an age when "information" rather than "knowledge" proliferates and when instant solutions to everything from the problem of self-esteem to space travel are considered our prerogative, it is important to discover again this element of mystery in the universe and in life.

In his story of Alexander the Great, the historian Arrian records the end of this remarkable man's life. Alexander had conquered the world while still young, but finally fell ill. His physicians cared for him and his priests prayed for him. It seemed inconceivable that this great man should not survive. But Arrian concludes this part of his account, "But the gods' command was made public, and soon afterward Alexander died—this being the better thing."[5] The "better thing" was to accept the mystery of the ultimate limitation of humans. Not even Alexander could transcend this human condition. There is only one God, and the writer of Kings writes in that conviction. In him, humans face an ultimate mystery whom they cannot control or manipulate. And in the history of Israel, it is his will which is being demonstrated.

Having witnessed the exile of a people once so blessed, and having felt the pain of bewilderment and confusion, the writer pulled his resources together to instruct, to condemn, and also to encourage. His knowledge of God is of a God whose disposition is one of grace, and on this he builds a platform for future hope. He is an encourager.

Much has been made in recent years of the work of the great literary figures of the Exile and of the postexilic period —men like the writer of Isaiah 40–55, Ezekiel, the chronicler, Ezra, Nehemiah, and the lesser-known prophets like Haggai and Zechariah and Malachi. They reconstruct a people, a faith, and a religion out of the loss of land, temple, and king. Ezekiel has been called "the pastor of the exiled congregation," and deservedly so. But it is the deuteronomist's masterful exposition of the past which provides the platform on which he can construct hope for the present and future.

NOTES

Preface

1. J. Ellul, *The Politics of God and the Politics of Man*, trans. G. W. Bromiley (Grand Rapids: Eerdmans, 1972).

Chapter 1 Introduction

1. S. R. Driver, *A Critical and Exegetical Commentary on Deuteronomy*, ICC (Edinburgh: T. & T. Clark, 1903). M. Weinfeld, *Deuteronomy and the Deuteronomistic School* (Oxford: Oxford University Press, 1972).

2. J. H. Hayes and P. K. Hooker, *A New Chronology for the Kings of Israel and Judah* (Atlanta: John Knox Press, 1988). Other chronological schemes exist, and comparisons are invited with S. J. DeVries "Chronology of the OT," *Interpreter's Dictionary of the Bible*, vol. 1 (Nashville: Abingdon, 1962), 580-90. J. Bright, *A History of Israel*, 3d ed. (Philadelphia: Westminster Press, 1981), 465-73 (based on the work of W. F. Albright).

3. R. Polzin, *Moses and the Deuteronomist* (New York: Seabury Press, 1980), 19.

Chapter 2 Kings

1. J. Ellul, *The Politics of God and the Politics of Man*, 18.

2. G. E. Mendenhall, "The Monarchy," *Interpretation* 29 (1975):160.

3. F. S. Frick, "King," *Harper's Bible Dictionary* (San Francisco: Harper and Row, 1985), 527.

95

Chapter 3 Prophets

1. G. von Rad, "The Deuteronomistic Theology of History in the Books of Kings," in *Studies in Deuteronomy*, trans. D. Stalker (London: SCM Press, 1953), 74–91.

2. Ibid., 78.

3. G. E. Mendenhall review of R. R. Wilson, *Prophecy and Society in Ancient Israel* (Philadelphia: Fortress Press, 1980) in *Biblical Archeologist* 44 (1981), 190.

Chapter 5 The Covenanted Land

1. W. Brueggemann, *The Land* (Philadelphia: Westminster Press, 1977), 71–89.

Chapter 6 Sin and Judgment

1. J. Goldingay, *Theological Diversity and the Authority of the Old Testament* (Grand Rapids: Eerdmans, 1987), 62.

Chapter 7 Hope and the Anger of God

1. R. W. Klein, *Israel in Exile: A Theological Interpretation* (Philadelphia: Fortress Press, 1979), 43.

2. B. T. Dahlberg, "Anger," in *Interpreter's Dictionary of the Bible*, vol. 1 (Nashville: Abingdon, 1962), 1:135.

3. A. Heschel, *The Prophets*, vol. 2 (New York: Harper and Row, 1960), 86.

4. R. P. Carroll, *From Chaos to Covenant: Prophecy in the Book of Jeremiah* (New York: Crossroads, 1981), 248.

5. R. Polzin, *Moses and the Deuteronomist*, 19.

Chapter 8 Conclusion

1. G. Savran, "1 and 2 Kings," in *The Literary Guide to the Bible*, eds. R. Alter and F. Kermode (Cambridge, Mass.: Harvard University Press, 1988), 146–64.

2. Ibid.

3. A. Heschel, *The Prophets*, vol. 1 (New York: Harper and Row, 1960), xii–xiii.

4. Ibid., xiii.

5. Arrian, *The Campaigns of Alexander*, trans. A. de Selincourt (Harmondsworth, U.K.: Penguin Books, 1971), 394.

BIBLIOGRAPHY

All quotations in the body of the text can be found in the various books listed below. Included in this list are those works cited in the text as well as others which may be of interest to the reader who would like to explore the general topics in more detail.

Aharoni, Y. *The Land of the Bible.* Tr. A. F. Rainey. 2d ed. Philadelphia: Westminster Press, 1979.

Arrian. *The Campaigns of Alexander.* Tr. A. de Selincourt. Harmondsworth: Penguin Books, 1971.

Blenkinsopp, J. *A History of Prophecy in Israel.* Philadelphia: Westminster Press, 1983. A good modern introduction to the prophets.

Brueggemann, W. *The Land.* Philadelphia: Westminster Press, 1977.

———. *The Prophetic Imagination.* Philadelphia: Westminster Press, 1978. One of the best popular introductions to the prophets.

Carroll, R. P. *From Chaos to Covenant: Prophecy in the Book of Jeremiah.* New York: Crossroads, 1981. A detailed study of the activity of the deuteronomists.

Driver, S. R. *A Critical and Exegetical Commentary on Deuteronomy.* ICC Edinburgh: T. & T. Clark, 1903.

Ellul, J. *The Politics of God and the Politics of Man.* Tr. G. W. Bromiley. Grand Rapids: Eerdmans, 1972.

Goldingay, J. *Theological Diversity and the Authority of the Old Testament.* Grand Rapids: Eerdmans, 1987. Goldingay treats the topic of the "people of God" as a test case in this interesting book.

Hayes, J. H., and P. K. Hooker. *A New Chronology for the Kings of Israel and Judah.* Atlanta: John Knox Press, 1988. This book provides the basis for the dates in the chart on pp. 8–9. The topic of Old Testament chronology is an extremely complicated one (see WBC 13:xxxviii–xliv), and this book offers a new and workable approach.

Heschel, A. *The Prophets.* 2 vols. New York: Harper and Row, 1960.

Hobbs, T. R. "2 Kings 1 and 2: Unity and Purpose," *Studies in Religion/Sciences Religieuses* 13 (1984) 327–34.

———. "The Search for Prophetic Consciousness: Some Comments on Method," *Biblical Theology Bulletin* 15 (1985): 136–41.

Klein, R. W. *Israel in Exile: A Theological Interpretation.* Philadelphia: Fortress Press, 1979.

Malina, B. J., and J. H. Neyrey. *Calling Jesus Names: The Social Value of Labels in Matthew.* Sonoma, Calif.: Polebridge Press, 1988. Apart from its intrinsic value, this book has an excellent series of charts on the differences between North American and Mediterranean culture. These differences are appealed to on many occasions in the present volume.

McCarthy, D. J. *Treaty and Covenant.* Atlanta: John Knox Press, 1972.

Mendenhall, G. E. "The Monarchy," *Interpretation* 29 (1975):155–70.

———. Review of R. R. Wilson, "Prophet and Society in Ancient Israel" in *Biblical Archeologist* 44 (1981):189–90.

Polzin, R. *Moses and the Deuteronomist.* New York: Seabury Press, 1980.

Pritchard, J. B., ed. *Ancient Near Eastern Texts Relating to the Old Testament.* Princeton: Princeton University Press, 1955.

Savran, G. "1 and 2 Kings" in *The Literary Guide to the Bible,* Eds. R. Alter and F. Kermode. Cambridge, Mass.: Harvard University Press, 1988, 146–64.

Tadmor, H., and M. Cogan. *II Kings: A New Translation with an Introduction and Commentary.* Anchor Bible 11. New York: Doubleday, 1988.

von Rad, G. "The Theology of History in the Books of Kings," in *Studies in Deuteronomy.* Tr. D. Stalker. London: SCM Press, 1953.

Weinfeld, M. *Deuteronomy and the Deuteronomistic School.* Oxford: Oxford University Press, 1972.